Gaining Heaven's PERSPECTIVE

A GUIDE TO HEARING AND SEEING THE VOICE OF GOD

JULIAN C. ADAMS

RIVER
PUBLISHING

River Publishing & Media Ltd
www.river-publishing.co.uk
info@river-publishing.co.uk

ISBN 978-1-908393-22-7

Contents

Dedication

This book is dedicated to two people who played a short but powerful role in my life. An apostle and a prophet. Both lived their lives to the full and gave their lives to the purposes of God in their generation. I do miss them both.

Simon Petitt
and
Anne Van Niekerk

What Others Are Saying...

Julian's remarkable gift of prophecy has been a huge blessing to many. His insight is matched by his love and tenderness. Many have experienced a fresh encounter with Jesus through his wonderful prophetic gift.

Terry Virgo
Founder of the Newfrontiers family of churches, Bible teacher and author.

I have always found Julian Adams' teaching on prophetic ministry stimulating and faith provoking. This book is an excellent example of this and both equips us and imparts faith to enjoy the presence of God and hear his voice.

David Devenish
Newfrontiers and Catalyst Team.

We live in a time when the gospel has been reduced to a trinity comprising Father, Son and me. This book will start you on a journey to discovering the full, panoramic work of the Holy Spirit – the Spirit who gloriously seals our salvation and affirms our adoption as sons and daughters. But also a Spirit who clothes us with power from on high, equipping us with many gifts as we serve Jesus in the building of His church.

David Capener
Church Planter/Leader, *Redeemer Central*, Belfast, UK

Julian has endeavored to stir faith in the believer for the release of the supernatural. As you learn to hear God in a new way, may heaven touch your earth, making the supernatural very real and natural!

Janet Brann-Hollis, *Ruach Ministries,* Johannesburg, South Africa

Activation is currently a popular word and the Julian I know is an activator of note. Dare I say, this is why God is using him in such remarkable ways in these days. As you read this book you will be motivated to become an activator, not just a reader (John 13:17).

Jeff Kidwell, Senior Pastor, *The Bay Community Church*, Cape Town, South Africa

Julian has tackled the complex and, at times, confusing subject of prophetic perspective with clarity and ease. His evident personal experience and integrity of life uniquely position him to write on this subject. The result: a book firmly grounded in scripture and practice that is a pleasure to read. He demystifies the subject of the prophetic and at the same time values the supernatural, resulting in the reader feeling encouraged to reach for more of God and more of His presence.

Lindsey Pettit, Restorative Justice Facilitator, Cape Town, South Africa

It's my privilege to call Julian my closest friend. Over the years I have seen him develop and grow in character, gifting and calling. He is a man of integrity and honour, with a passion for the church. But what inspires me most about Julian is his constant pursuit of God's presence, his insatiable desire for Jesus. Julian has steadily been putting this book together for the past few years and he has asked me on occasion to give it a read. I have seen Julian's own understanding of the prophetic grow and deepen over this time, so that the book you now hold contains great insight and practical help, richly seasoned by Julian's own experiences. It is dense in wisdom and is a great tool for leaders and those wanting to grow in the prophetic.

Sean Butler, Church Planter, Middle East

Julian is a great friend and a true Father to me. There is very little in the prophetic and in life that I have not learnt from him! I can think of no one better to teach on the prophetic than Julian, as he lives a radical life that embodies what the prophetic is all about – showing God's lavishly abundant love, grace and favour to the world. If you can catch that from this book, then you're well on your way to growing in your prophetic gift. What I love about this book is that it makes the prophetic so accessible for everyone, rather than a super-spiritual, mystical practice for a select few. At the same time it captures the destiny-shaping, life-changing power of heaven's perspective breaking into earth.

David Child, Businessman and Worship Co-ordinator, *The Bay Community Church*, Cape Town, South Africa.

Thank You

Wow! I can't believe that this book is finally in print. Many have asked me to write a book on prophecy and I have constantly said, "no."

God, however, had other plans. After hearing Dr. Mark Stibbe speak on "the writing anointing" and having received numerous words about writing, this is my first attempt.

I wish I could say this was all my effort, but really this book began in the heart of my parents, Chris and Bubbles (as many affectionately call her) when they dedicated me to Jesus while I was still in my mother's tummy. Prophetic words they received and prayed over me were stewarded by them before I could even prophesy. For their passion, zeal and life-long integrity, I honour them. Dad and Mom, thank you, you are the platform I stand on each time I preach or prophesy.

I have so many people I want to thank: my family, brothers, sister (in-law, too) and nieces. I love you lots and thank you for loving me with all my craziness.

Janet Brann-Hollis, you were the prophet who spoke the things I now do. I love how you have mentored me, albeit from afar. I am looking forward to many more ministry times together.

Jeff and Viv Kidwell and The Bay Community Church: my season of eldership with you helped shape all that I am today. This really is the fruit of your experiences in God.

Terry and Wendy Virgo: my year spent with you changed my life. I'm glad you taught me about grace; where would I be without it?

And then to many who have loved me, prayed for me and supported me. Names can mean little to others in a book like this, but I am putting your names here because you have helped change many lives through your deep friendship with me:

Sean and Shannon Butler, Carla Adams, Richard and Monique Glass, Jane Spengler, David Child, Justin and Renata Sherwin, Simon and Caroline Holley, Steve and Heather Oliver, Brandon de Beer and Jeremy and Anne Simpkins. Your names mean the world to me. Thanks for shaping my life through being generous with yours.

Julian Adams

Foreword

Julian Adams is a gift from God to us. His depth of revelation, sound approach to scripture, love for the church and care for individuals have helped set a new culture for the prophetic in our movement of churches that is making a massive impact.

Not only does he hear from God with wonderful accuracy, both for individuals and the church, he also has a passion to equip and train others to do the same. I've been so blessed to get to know him and to see that he is the real thing!

Julian is a man of character and integrity who not only does the stuff but helps and inspires others to do the same. You will be blessed by reading this book!

Simon Holley
Lead Elder, *The Kings Arms*, Bedford, United Kingdom

Introduction

I remember with great clarity sitting at the feet of a prophet called Janet Brann. The room was electric and the words she gave were so accurate that there were loud gasps and chuckles each time she prophesied with incredible depth and insight over someone. I fell in love with Jesus on that day in a way I never had before. I was just a nine-year-old boy then. I discovered for myself that day that God had a plan for my life – one that would take me to the nations and see many thousands of people impacted because of His goodness. Little did I know that the very thing she was doing, one day I would do. The prophetic ministry began for me that day. I began to hear, feel and see God's voice at work and I loved it.

In fact, I still love it!

This book is not intended to be a theological exposition on signs, wonders and prophecy. Nor is it intended to be a manual or step-by-step guide to accessing heavenly revelation. It is meant to be like a movie trailer. Simply put, this book is a prelude to the movie – a taste tester before the main meal.

God has prepared some incredible experiences that you and I can walk in. My prayer is that this book will whet your appetite for a deeper encounter with Jesus. All satisfaction and joy is wrapped up in who He is. He is all prophecy fulfilled. He is the spirit of prophecy (Revelation 19:10).

It was not until recently that I felt like I had much to say on the subject of the prophetic. That was until I started seeing (as opposed to just hearing) what the prophetic ministry is all about. I have often said that there must be more than the "lightweight" and "low-level" prophetic ministry that I have seen on display in some of our charismatic churches.

Please, do not get me wrong: it's not that I despise prophecy, which would be in blatant disobedience to scripture. It's just that prophecy has been reduced to such a blasé gift that we seem to have lost its clear supernatural nature. We seem to have reduced prophecy to words about cows in the meadows and sunflowers in the fields.

Forgive me for my tongue-in-cheek remarks, but that hardly makes for meetings where sinners will fall down and exclaim that God is in the house!

New Testament prophecy was treated with a sense of awe – as if God were speaking directly to the people (which He was!). In fact, it was treated with such awe that Paul gave instructions to "weigh the prophetic word" (1 Corinthians 14:29).

This was more than just the eldership checking to see if the word was right or wrong. It was required to be weighed because if it was from God, they would be required to respond to the word. Beyond personal or corporate prophetic words, we seem to have lost those prophets who experience and enjoy prophetic encounters with God.

Yet the reality of revelation is wide open to us and the Bible is full of examples of men and women who encountered God in extraordinary ways.

Although these can be seen as "extraordinary" encounters, still God has made them available to us in an ordinary world. The promise of the kingdom of God is that although it is unseen to the natural man, it is gloriously revealed to the one whose spirit has been made alive in Jesus. This means that any born-again believer has access to God-encounters and prophetic experiences that are out of this world.

He has lots more for you to enjoy here on this planet and you can have it now. If this book makes you hungry for more of Jesus – if it drives you to a place of revelation by the Spirit – then I will be happy!

I hope it does. Enjoy this journey into the supernatural. God loves it when we step out in faith.

Having gifts that differ according to the grace given to us, let us use them: if prophecy, in proportion to our faith. Romans 12:6.

Much Love,
Julian Adams

1
Living Under An Open Heaven

Therefore, brothers, since we have confidence to enter the holy place by the blood of Jesus, by the new and living way that he opened for us through the curtain, that is, through his flesh, and since we have a great priest over the house of God, let us draw near with a true heart in full assurance of faith, with our hearts sprinkled clean from an evil conscience and our bodies washed with pure water. Let us hold fast the confession of our hope without wavering, for he who promised is faithful.
Hebrews 10:19-23

God has called us to be a people who live in the realm of the supernatural as a normal part of our daily life. We are a new community, a people of the Spirit. Many people do not know how to access or experience this realm of the Spirit. In fact, many

Christians have never understood their salvation inheritance and the incredible resources available to them to live a powerful, overcoming life. It seems to me that for many Christians, a fresh revelation of who they are in Jesus is needed.

Jesus modeled and made a way for us to live that is *supernaturally natural*. We are, according to John 3:6-8, born of the Spirit and therefore live from the realm of the Spirit. We have to learn from Jesus how we ought to live. Jesus prayed, *"let your will be done on earth as it is in heaven."* He lived in a duality from heaven to earth .

In John 3 we see that Jesus says,

If I have told you earthly things and you do not believe, how can you believe if I tell you heavenly things? No one has ascended into heaven except he who descended from heaven, the Son of Man who is in heaven.

He lived in a duality.

Later in the book of John he says things like, *"I do nothing unless I see my father do it"* and *"My Father who is in heaven has been working until now, and even now the Son is working."*

Jesus modeled a life of living from heaven to earth. He came from heaven to earth and brought with Him heaven's culture and the rule and reign of God. If we are to see the full outworking of what He started, we have to do it the way Jesus did it.

He is our great example. Jesus lived under an open he
We read that at His baptism the heavens were torn open and
the Father's affirmation was poured out on Him. That was the
inauguration of His ministry and from that point on He began to
heal the sick and do mighty miracles. If we are to live like Him
we need to understand how He lived under that open heaven.

I have heard many teachings on open heavens and walking in
the miraculous. Most of the time, I have walked away feeling
condemned and unable to enter into all that Jesus has for me. It
seemed like a lot of hard work with far too much fasting and self-
denial. It did not line up with a biblical understanding of grace.

So I began to study up on what heaven is really like. The first
thing we need to understand is Jesus' theology of heaven. This is
very different from the way that most understand heaven today.
Most believers have a theology of heaven that has no effect on
the way they live. This is because they think of Heaven only in the
context of the day that we die! If we were to ask many Christians
today what they think about Heaven, the answer would likely be
"I can't wait to get there one day."

While I can't wait to get to heaven too, heaven is much broader
and deeper than that.

When Jesus came to earth, He came with a message saying,
"Repent for the kingdom of Heaven is at hand." He was declaring
a change had come. He was ushering in a new reality regarding
the presence of heaven. He was saying, "Change the way you

think about heaven. Do not hold onto the same old ideas about heaven you are used to, because heaven is now within arm's reach."

Heaven is at hand. N.T. Wright says, "God's Kingdom in the preaching of Jesus refers not to post-mortem destiny, not to our escape from this world into another one, but it is God's sovereign rule coming 'on earth as it is in heaven'." He goes on to say that Heaven "is a picture of pre-sent reality, the heavenly dimension of our present life. Heaven, in the bible is regularly not a future destiny, but the other, hidden dimension of our ordinary life – God's dimension if you like."

To the Jew who heard Jesus' words was presented a radical new way of thinking about heaven. Until then, the Jews would have thought of heaven through the mindset of the Old Testament prophets. They would know that heaven was and is the domain of the Living God. It was where Yahweh dwelt – the God who reveals Himself to those whom He chooses.

They would have known that heaven is where the throne of Yahweh is established and where angels worship Him daily. They would have remembered Isaiah's vision of the throne of heaven. They would have remembered the pleas of the prophet crying out for a radical change in their nation, saying, "Lord, that you would tear open the heavens and come down." They would have known the scriptures which promised that the window of heaven would open up if they brought the tithe into the store house.

Tear open the heavens and come down

They would also know that they had no access into heaven because of their sin, which separated them from the domain of God. They could not enter into heaven, the realm of God. They could not enter into the presence of God because of the stain of sin. Only He who is holy can "ascend the hill of the Lord".

This was further reinforced by the way the temple was constructed. It all pointed to the fact that no one could enter into the presence of God. The dwelling place of His presence was impenetrable, except for once a year for the one priest who went into the holy of holies.

Heaven is the dwelling place of God, Yahweh, the Great I AM. But Jesus came and declared, "The kingdom of heaven is at hand" and everything changed.

He was radical. His message was so radical that it got Him crucified. This is the good news that He brought: "The domain of the Great I AM is closer than you think; it is within arm's reach!"

He was saying to the people, "You see that temple? You see this priesthood? It's all changed because I am here. It will all become obsolete; it will all pass away because I will establish a new and living way, so that anyone can access and live in the realm of heaven. Anyone can come and approach the living God. Anyone can come close to Yahweh. Anyone can enter His realm!"

The writer to the Hebrews understood this and with much insight he helps us understand the right of access we have into

Jesus declared "the kingdom of heaven is at hand"
(apart for)

the very presence and realm of God. We get to live under an open heaven – the place where God dwells.

 In order for us to fully understand our access, we need to understand what Jesus accomplished for us at the cross. We will have to understand a bit more of the Jewish mindset if we are to walk into all that God has for us. Many people approach the presence of God through the lens of the Old Testament with its rules and regulations. In fact, most of the church has lived with this mindset for years and the result is that they don't enter into living under the favour of an open heaven. There is a new and living way for us to enter into. We cannot camp in the old mindset any more.

At Bible school we were taught to approach God through the template of the temple worship system. All this did for me was to bring condemnation. The writer to the Hebrews gives us clues as to how the Jewish temple system worked. This is a short explanation of how people were to enter into the place where God dwells.

It was a physical representation of how they were to approach God in a spiritual reality.

Firstly, they built what is called a "tabernacle". This is the word for "dwelling place" and it is where God dwelt with His people. This tabernacle had specific dimensions and each thing in it was a foreshadowing – a picture of what it would be like for us to be "in Christ".

There were huge bronze gates that people would enter through. It took many men just to open these gates. If you were a gentile this was about as far as you could come. You could only enter into the outer court. That was it for you. No other access. The Jew could then enter into the inner court, where the sacrifices would be made and the priest would have to go through a series of cleansing rituals. This is all a picture of what Christ did for us. He became the sacrifice for us and provided cleansing from all our sin.

At each point there would be a door that the priest would have to go through. They would then come into the holy place. This was as far as the ordinary priest could go.

Then, once a year, the high priest would access the most holy place. There would be a curtain. One might expect another door, but there was simply a curtain to pass through – a temporary veil between man and God. God's design was never an expression of intent to remain separate from man.

As the high priest entered into the most holy place he would see blood all over the floor – a product of many years of blood sprinkled on the floor to atone for sins. This was a picture of the blood of Jesus.

As he approached the throne of mercy and came near to the mercy seat, he remained secure because the blood was sprinkled before every step he made – covering all his sin. This is what our High Priest did when He went ahead of us, shedding His blood so that we could confidently come close to the throne of God, knowing that our sin was covered by the blood of Jesus. He was the sacrificial Lamb for us! The priest would then approach the mercy seat to find the mercy of God.

These things all present a picture of how we are able to approach God. But if we stopped there we would find ourselves bound by legalism, with no real way of enjoying free access to the favour of God. Many people are still stuck in the old model of approaching God.

The truth is that when Jesus came, something changed forever. We read of Jesus that at His baptism that the heavens were torn open. That single event released a deluge of Holy Spirit activity in Jesus' life. When Jesus died, the curtain in the temple was torn open from top to bottom, never to be closed again. This is the clearest statement that the old way of approaching God and living under an open Heaven was changed forever.

Because the very flesh of Jesus was torn open, we now have free access into the most holy place in heaven! Access is now never based on what we have done, but on the sprinkled blood of the eternal Lamb who has gone ahead, tearing in His own flesh every hindrance to entering into and living under an open Heaven.

The heavens are open!

Later on we see Stephen saying in Acts 7,

Behold, I see the heavens opened and the Son of Man sitting on his throne!

Notice Stephen did not say, "I see the heavens opening." He said they are opened! That word "open" is an eternal state. The heavens will never close. Peter, in his encounter in Acts 10, had the same experience where he saw the heavens opened – they were not simply opening. They were opened and he had access.

John, in his encounter saw a door open in the heavens. He simply engaged in a realm that was as real as this earthly realm. He was entering into heaven's open door. Malachi got only a window, but we have a door that is wide open! Under the old covenant the heavens were opened by God's initiation. But under the new covenant the heavens are open *continually*!

So how does this affect the way we live day to day? How we think about the reality of heaven and about our access to the presence of God affects how we live in this world. When we have a grasp on the reality of our free access into heaven, into the most holy place, we come into a new understanding of how God interacts with us in this present world.

Let not your hearts be troubled. Believe in God; believe also in me. In my Father's house are many rooms. If it were not so, would I have told you that I go to prepare a place for you? And if I go and prepare a place for you, I will come again and will take you to myself, that where I am you may be also. John 14:1-5

Jesus has now gone ahead of us and has made a way for us to enter into God's domain. He has made a way into the most holy place. He is the first born from amongst the dead. He is our prototype. We now have free access into heaven. Where the heavens were closed to those of the old covenant, the new covenant has opened heaven to us.

This is why Jesus so clearly and provocatively prophesied the demise of the temple, saying that He would raise up another temple – a living temple – in three days (John 2:18-22). He was clearly saying that this old way of approaching God with all its legalism and ritual would be torn down.

In fact, the curtain of His flesh was torn in two and we now have free access into the very heaven of heavens (Hebrews 10:19-23). The glorious truth is that we have access. There is a person in heaven called Jesus who has made a way for us to come now, so that where He is we may be also!

The problem for most Christians is that they live in both expressions of the covenant. It is clear to me that the vast majority of the church is bound by teaching that causes us to approach worship through the mindset of the old pattern, thereby blocking us off from intimacy with the Father.

Remember how Adam and Eve tried to cover themselves with their own attempt at clothing in the form of fig leaves? All this did was to hide them from the presence of God. It did not deal with their sin or shame (Genesis 3:8-10). James wrote that, "A *double-minded man receives nothing from the Lord"* (James 1:7-8), so if we live in both expressions of the covenant we forfeit our enjoyment of all the new covenant has to offer. This is why Hebrews tells us that the worship offered under the old covenant was not enough to clear a man of his sin – thus the need for a yearly sacrifice. That old way of approaching God only served to reinforce the separation between man and God (Hebrews 10:1-10). Under the new covenant we get to enter into the realms of heaven and live from there.

Many people can recognise a demonic presence. They will sense an evil presence and have a sick feeling in their tummy or a sense of pressure around their heads when there is demonic power present. This is because people have learned to discern when darkness has come near. How much more we need to learn how to discern when God's kingdom comes near!

Tom Wright says, "Heaven and earth, it seems, are not after all poles apart, needing to be separated forever when all the children of heaven have been rescued from this wicked world. Nor are they simply different ways of looking at the same thing. NO: they are different, radically different; but they are made for each other."

Thank God for Jesus! His blood has made a new and living way for us to engage in the realm of God's domain. Heaven is open now. It will never close. I no longer need to pray for an open heaven, because it is continually open to me. Never again will I know a day of no access into the presence of God. Not only that, but I am seated with Him and in Him in the heavenly places (Ephesians 2:6). My whole perspective is now changed. I live from Heaven to Earth! Just like Jesus, I will never have a day when heaven is closed to me.

Jesus overcame death for us. He won the final victory. The Bible says that we have all sinned and fallen short of the glory of God. The glory that was lost in the Garden of Eden is now restored in Jesus.

Where heaven and earth met in harmony as the presence of God was unveiled, now in Jesus, heaven and earth meet. When Jesus was raised from the dead, He was not separated from His body. He was still clothed in a physical body. His body could be touched and He could eat. He then ascended into heaven. There is a man with a physical, glorified body in the undiluted presence of the glory of God. His promise to us is that where He is, we may be also.

How do we get into these rooms of heaven? Through Jesus, the one who has gone ahead of us and lives to make intercession for us. The realm of the supernatural is open to us because of Jesus. We get to enter through Him, right into the presence of God.

At His baptism, Jesus had the Spirit of God rest on Him. It was that resting of the Spirit on Him that authenticated His sonship. In the same way, in John 14 Jesus promises us that we will receive the Holy Spirit and that He will draw us into a radical relationship with the Father. In fact, it's how we will know that we are in Christ and that Christ is in the Father. Being in Christ is the access point to the realm of heaven. He is the way we engage in the supernatural!

2
Undomesticated

By the spring of 2007 I had been living in England for eight months, serving our *Newfrontiers* family of churches. Before then I had been serving my local church, *The Bay Community Church* in South Africa, as an elder. I came from a good church in Cape Town and we had seen a number of healings and God-encounters. *The Bay Community Church* are a radical bunch who really know how to press into the presence of the Holy Spirit!

While in the UK, I had travelled to many different churches preaching, prophesying, speaking at elders' meetings and conferences. It was fun and having the opportunity to see so many churches was a real privilege. For a guy like me who had never been exposed to many churches internationally, it was thrilling to see what God was doing in the UK.

After months of travelling, however, I realised I was getting tired. It had been my first time conducting travelling ministry at such an intense pace!

So I booked myself in at a conference at a church in Birmingham. They were hosting a couple called Rolland and Heidi Baker who lead Iris Ministries. They are a church planting and mercy ministry that is affecting sub-Saharan Africa and beyond. They are a dynamic couple and I knew I was in for a real treat in the presence of God.

It had been a long time since I had been in a situation where I could just enjoy the presence of God. One evening I went up to receive prayer. While I was standing in the ministry line I felt slightly irritated that it was taking so long for someone to come and pray for me! Just as I was about to go back and sit down, someone came over to me. It was these next few minutes that would change my view on the prophetic forever.

As this person prayed for me, the power of God began to flow through me like electricity. The sense of His presence was overwhelming and I knew Jesus was so close to me. As the presence of God began to increase on my body, I fell to the ground. It was as if I could no longer stand the intensity of His closeness and my body became weak and I fell to the floor. As this happened I was aware that my physical senses were being affected. It seemed as if the sound in the room was decreasing and eventually faded to a mumbling background noise.

Something different was happening. I had not experienced this before. I kept sensing the love of God like warm liquid all over me. I was also aware that it seemed to me as if the physical world was suspended and, as I fell to the ground, I kept on falling. It felt as if I was falling through thick air and I became aware that I was in another room. The experience I was having is called a trance. God spoke to people like this in the Bible (Acts 10:9).

It was exhilarating! I knew God had brought me to this place because He wanted to speak to me. As I walked into the room I was drawn to walk down a wall on the right hand side of me. As I walked through this walkway I came to an entrance to another room. Standing at the door I saw two angels looking down at me. They did not speak to me, yet the smile on their faces seemed to be a message to me. They were incredible to look at: tall, strong and covered in light. As they looked down at me and smiled, I sensed them encouraging me to go into the next room. I clearly felt like they knew this was about destiny for me.

As I walked into this room I was unaware of anything else other than the huge bed that was right in the centre of the room. This huge wooden bed had detailed carvings on it. It seemed to be an antique. I climbed onto this bed as as I did so, a rest came on me unlike anything I had experienced. I felt the Lord speak to me about ministering from a place of rest. I knew the Lord wanted to highlight this to me. I had become dry and weary from ministry. Serving out of your own strength and striving does not produce the kind of fruit that comes from rest.

As I lay on the bed, I felt the most incredible rest come to me. It felt like a deep satisfaction and joy flooded me right to the core of my bones! It had an effervescent effect on me. I felt like I had so much energy and strength. It was completely exhilarating. No earthly holiday could equate to it!

As I stretched out on the bed, God began to speak to me. During this encounter I could see so clearly, I could hear intensely, smell acutely, and feel things in a heightened way. Although I never saw God or Jesus during this time, I could sense His presence in the room. He stayed in a particular area and it was as if His form was concentrated in that area. As He spoke to me I felt a oneness with Him that I had never experienced before.

God began to speak to me about learning to rest in who He is and ministering from that place. As He began to encourage me to prophesy out of the bigness of His glory, I suddenly became aware of a large eagle in the corner of the room on a perch with a chain tied to its claw.

My heart began to race as a fear filled my heart. It was the hugest eagle I had ever seen. Its claws were sharp and his chest was pushed right out. His eyes, oh my word, his eyes were intensely fiery and blazing with passion. It was all absorbing to look at. God clearly and strongly said to me, "Son, I have brought you here to talk to you about the new shape and coming season of the prophetic ministry." A holy sense of fear and attention filled me as I heard those piercing words.

God began to speak to me and said, "Son, for too long the prophetic ministry has been placed on a perch. For too long it has been on show for people to look at and be amazed by. It is time to un-domesticate the prophetic ministry. No longer is it simply to sit on a perch in the church building. I want to bring a release to the prophetic ministry!"

At this point I heard a great crack as the chains of this eagle broke off. It was terrifying! I knew that a bird this large could do much damage. As I watched, the eagle began to spread its wings. The span of his wings was majestic. It was unbelievably beautiful with the most intense colours I had ever seen. The sound that it made as it began to lift its voice was almost ear-splitting. Again, God spoke to me saying,

"Son, I want to strip off man's attempt to domesticate prophetic encounters. No longer will man's ideas be a covering to the prophetic, but my glory will. Even as you see the span of this eagle's wings, so will I restore glory to the prophetic that will be a covering which will span far and wide."

"Eagles are meant to fly high and I am restoring to the church prophetic encounters, so that it will not be possible to put them into neat boxes of predictability and the safe confines of intellectual thinking. Eagles are meant to fly high, and it's in that place of catching the wind of my Spirit that they see the land. It's in that place of flying high that they see the spoil. It's in that place that they see the enemy and swoop down to destroy his plans and designs. Don't be surprised as I restore the realms of the seer prophet back to the church. I want my church to build again out of the place of revelation. Revelation from my Son for my glory!"

"In this season, the prophetic ministry will see further and clearer than ever before and it will lift up a cry like that of an eagle. That cry will fill the valley of indecision with clarity and decisiveness so that my church can move into all that she is called to. I want you to know that My glory will be a covering. Not man's ideas, not man's control. It will be my glory which will cover all-in-all as I release a new direction and shape to the prophetic ministry in these last days!"

My lasting impression of this encounter, which lasted for about half an hour, was the passionate intensity of the eagle's eyes. There was a determination to fly and to see the heights and depths for which it was created.

This experience has left me desperate for God to restore the prophetic ministry in a biblical and radical way. I never thought I would start a book off by relaying a subjective experience. I love the Bible. I love books (especially books about prophetic ministry) to be clearly full of biblical truth and explanation. I love it when books are clearly theological, with real meat in them. So starting like this is not really my style.

However, I did because the Bible is full of experiences. In fact, the Bible came out of prophetic experiences as people encountered the Holy Spirit and wrote about it! The Bible is filled with the experiences of others and if we are to be truly biblical it is not good enough to be satisfied with a theological and intellectual gospel. It must be experiential, too.

This, I believe, is true of the prophetic too. In these days God is restoring the eyes of the church in order to see clearly what He is doing. The church was birthed through prophetic encounters and I believe it is sustained and propelled by prophetic experiences. If we ignore these, the church will simply go blind and lose its ability to see from heaven's perspective.

As I began to study the Bible and get to grips with the role of the prophetic in the church, I found the things I could not ignore were the incredible prophetic encounters people had that shaped and moved the church.

I think of the outpouring of the Holy Spirit upon the early church (Acts 2). It was a response to the prophetic word spoken years earlier by the prophet Joel. It also carried a prophetic element in that Peter prophesied about a generation who would come into more of these experiences. People spoke in tongues, others heard them speak in their own native tongue, flames of fire rested on them and sounds were heard from heaven like that of wind! This is highly experiential.

Peter's life was characterized by some incredible experiences. In Acts 5:1-11 he received prophetic insight about Ananias and Sapphira's deceitfulness. This brought a holy fear upon the church and seemed to open the door to even more signs and wonders. He had an angel appear to him a number of times (Acts 5:19; 12:7-10) and the early church seemed to consider angelic encounters common place. In one incident they argued with a young girl because although she believed Peter was outside, they insisted it was only his angel (Acts 12:15). I want to know why, even if it was an angel, did they not invite him inside?!

Peter also had some incredible visions and trances. The trance Peter had in Acts 10:10 opened up the gentile world to the church and began the fulfillment of another prophetic word – that from the nation of Israel all the nations of the earth would be blessed (Genesis 22:17-18). Peter responded to heaven's desire to see all men saved and, as a result, we gentiles get to enter into Abraham's promise! This was a watershed moment for the church. It changed the way church was done from this point. A completely new "normal" was introduced because of Peter's encounter.

Let's not forget Philip and his daughters who prophesied. Philip's experience of signs and wonders and his encounter with an angel provided the platform of breakthrough for Africa to hear the gospel as he led the Ethiopian eunuch to the Lord (Acts 8). Again, this seemingly private encounter with God opened up a whole new nation for the church to evangelise!

Then there is Paul, who had some incredible encounters with heaven. He heard an audible voice from heaven, was struck down by a supernatural force, blinded, healed from his blindness, filled with the Holy Spirit, received various visions, was taken up into heaven and received the gospel of grace by personal revelation from Jesus! Imagine that! Jesus came to Paul personally and revealed the good news of His kingdom (Galatians 1:11-12). What did that look like? What we do know is that this personal revelation resulted in the bulk of the New Testament writings being produced by Paul. His revelation of Jesus is still providing revelation for others through his writings.

These are just a few of accounts from the book of Acts of how God opened heaven in order to change the church. Time and space will not permit me to list the many prophetic encounters that shaped history, the church and many individual lives. As I look at the incredible progress we are making to restore the church to its original mandate, I am concerned that whilst we have amazing courses on how to grow the church, how to prophesy more, and how to find our personal destiny, we are still not seeing churches and individuals released into their God-given call and blueprint for their lives.

And I tell you, you are Peter, and on this rock I will build my church, and the gates of hell shall not prevail against it. Matthew 16:18

Some people would argue that the five-fold ministry gifts died out with the last apostles. The truth is, however, that the church has not come into perfection and, until that happens, God will keep on releasing these gifts (Ephesians 4:11-12).

We understand that the church is built upon the *"foundation of the apostles and prophets"* (Ephesians 2:20). What does this actually mean? I believe that part of the answer is found in the scriptures we have just read above.

Prophets especially have the privilege of bringing revelation. Jesus says an incredible thing to Peter as he responds correctly to the question Jesus asks about His identity. Peter says, "You are the Son of God." Jesus' response is: "On this rock I will build my Church." Now what is the "rock" Jesus is talking about? Is it Peter, like the Catholics believe? Or is it simply Jesus in His historical setting? I believe the key is found in these words:

And Jesus answered him, "Blessed are you, Simon Bar-Jonah! For flesh and blood has not revealed this to you, but my father who is in heaven!" Matthew 16:17

The key is revelation! Peter did not acquire this knowledge through his own ability, the culmination of various theological studies. It came to him by revelation. And it is this revelation: *Jesus, the Son of God.*

This is both final and ongoing. Final in the sense that there is no other foundation we can build on apart from Christ. Nothing other than that revealed in the scriptures about who Jesus is.

Of course, all other revelation must be built upon and indeed submitted to Christ as He is revealed in the Bible. There is, however, a sense in which this Son of God is still speaking and revealing Himself. He seems to be showing Himself strong in all sorts of places. For example, in many of the Muslim world contexts people are receiving visitations from Jesus supernaturally. This is then ongoing revelation. Jesus is still speaking to His church and longs for her to be led by his voice!

To them God chose to make known how great among the Gentiles are the riches of the glory of this mystery, which is Christ in you, the hope of glory. Colossians 1:27

Living as a people of the future, a people who respond to the revelation of Jesus, is really about demonstrating a glorious mystery. Before you think I might be drifting off to gnostic thought, I simply mean that we are called to live as a reflection of that which has been revealed in the person of Jesus. The truth is that behind every mystery is a substance that has always been there – it just has not yet been revealed.

It is not that I am looking for a new revelation of some deep mystery; it's that I want to see fresh revelation of a mystery that has been hidden for eternity.

For example, I have often wondered how some card tricks are performed by sleight of hand. It has been a mystery to me for many years. But having recently met a young man who does these sleight of hand tricks, I now know how some of them work. He revealed to me something that was always there, I had just not seen it.

I believe there are treasures in God's Word that we need fresh revelation on in order to live as those who have tasted and seen the kingdom which is now breaking in on the world. Paul's antidote to the gnostic heresy that the church in Colosse was into, was simply to direct them to heavenly activity.

He did not say "Get more theology." He did not try to make them a bit more earth-bound. He said, *"If then you have been raised with Christ, seek the things that are above, where Christ is, seated at the right hand of God. Set your minds on things that are above, not on things that are on earth"* (Colossians 3:1-2). He is not simply saying, "Set your mind on Christ", although that is clearly the point. He says, "Set your minds on *things above.*" He tells them to shift their focus away from the earth and onto heavenly activity.

This, I believe, is key if we are to enjoy fresh encounters that make a difference to our churches and our lives. The word of God is the purest form of prophecy and always takes precedence over subjective prophetic experiences. We must not and cannot attribute the same authority to prophecy as we do to the Holy Scriptures. We will fall dangerously into deception if we do. However, God wants to speak to us in order to prepare His church for effective ministry.

The simplicity of it all is that Christ in you! The key to being positioned for revelation is found in the work of salvation. I now have free access to heaven's courts. Some would say that we have to do spiritual warfare before we can enter into the fullness of an open heaven. I believe that because I am in Him I have a perpetual open heaven. After all, He is seated at the right hand of the Father! This then is the position I come from when I want to enjoy the mystery of the kingdom. In Him all things are revealed.

Positioned for revelation

Heart

1. *Prophetic revelation begins with the heart*

How do we position ourselves to receive revelation from God? I believe that all revelation is sovereignly initiated, yet it is important to realize that we can position ourselves to come into increased revelation. We must remember that it is not the type of revelation one receives, but the fact that we do receive revelation that is important.

Often we can place an emphasis on whether or not we are having a trance or angelic visitations, and then rank them in degrees of importance. The prophetic is not about this and should never be treated with this attitude. We are after the heart of God. We want people to come into an encounter with His heart.

Prophetic revelation begins with the heart. We have to realise that the condition of our heart will determine the yield of fruitfulness in this area (Luke 8: 4-8).

Your private devotion sets the context from which revelation flows. The Bible tells us that the degree to which we receive the word of the kingdom in our hearts will determine the yield of its harvest. We see four types of soil described in these verses. The first is like a pathway, which speaks of an unregenerate heart.

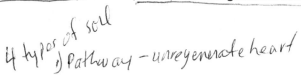

4 types of soul
1) Pathway – unregenerate heart

It says that the word is trampled underfoot. It is not treated with care or diligence and is lost.

2) Rocky path - hard heart

The second is a rocky path, which speaks of a hard heart. It is also interesting to note that Jesus says when testing comes, because the seed is not rooted into the ground, it is destroyed.

3) Soil overridden w/ thorns and thistles

The next type of soil the Bible talks about is one that is overridden with thorns and thistles. This speaks of an uncultivated garden where "strongholds" (these type of plants choke the life of the word out of the seed) are left to grow wild and mess things up.

4) Good Soil - receives and produces

Then finally we read about "good soil". This is a heart cultivated and tendered – soil that receives and produces. It is also interesting to note that the Word is being compared to a seed. This is because it has potential wrapped up in it. It will only come into the fullness of its potential in the right context. Apart from that it will not produce lasting fruit. This is true of the prophetic word. It produces fruit in the right conditions.

The Word is compared to a seed

2. Training our senses

The next way we can be positioned for revelation is to train our senses. Our bodies are designed to recognize and enjoy the presence of God. We can taste, see, smell, hear and touch in the Spirit! We must train our senses, so that we do not miss our time of visitation (Hebrews 5:14).

The western world is so often caught up in a cerebral understanding of God such that we miss engaging with Him in the reality of our body. Jesus did. He spoke of power flowing from Him (Mark 5:30). Luke tells of a time when the power of the Lord was present to heal (Luke 5:17). I wonder what was different that made Luke, a doctor and clearly very detailed person, make that statement. How did he recognize that the power of God was there?

The point is simply that God will often use what is seemingly ordinary and turn it into something extraordinary. For example, God used the hem of Jesus' garment to heal people. An ordinary robe became the conduit for God's power. Something ordinary became extraordinary! We must learn to sense and know His presence. Often in a meeting my left hand will start to burn. It will be a sign to me that there is a healing anointing in the room. Do I need it every time before I pray? No. However, when I do sense it, I step into a realm of faith I had previously not been in before.

Sometimes the Lord will cause a literal longing to occur in the pit of my stomach when he wants extended time with me. Do I wait for these before I go and love on Him? Absolutely not. Yet when He calls me to be with Him in these times, they are often filled with revelation. It is not hard to look through the scriptures to see that God engages with people in a holistic way: spirit, mind and body. He wants us to experience Him. For those who say we should not base our Christianity on an experience, I would say even the word of God came to us by men who were *"moved by the Spirit"* (2 Peter 1:21). It was birthed out of a Holy Spirit experience!

Holy Spirit

Lord teach me to Sense and Know your Presence.

Every part of me engages with Jesus! My body is designed to recognise the presence of God. It's what causes us to come into the fullness of life. It is how we are led by the Spirit. I say this simply to say, the Bible came to us by revelation. Nothing can equal that and it is the highest form of revelation. Any revelation that is contrary to the word of God is false and will lead to deception no matter how great it is. However, the people who wrote scripture were just people like us, receiving powerful revelation from the Spirit.

I was preaching at a church in Swindon, UK, when a couple came up to seek direction about a pending move from one country to another. As I stood to prophesy I could suddenly smell maple syrup. I could have ignored it and put it down to a "sugar low", yet I sensed God was in it. As I said what I smelled the whole church gasped and then the couple told me that Canada was the very place they wanted to go. It served as a confirmation to them.

3. Read about God-encounters

Lastly, we can study and meditate on biblical encounters. There are many encounters recorded in the Bible that point to encounters we could have – things like portals, open heavens, standing in the counsel of heaven (Psalm 25:14; 106:13,15) and angelic visions! These develop faith in our hearts and cause us to long for more of God.

In addition, when we base our experiences on biblical principles it provides a safeguard for us, which is so important if we want to grow in healthy prophetic ministry. The point is this: Jesus promised that there were "things" He longed to share with His disciples. He promised that when the Holy Spirit came He would reveal them to us (John 16:12-15).

I was conducting a meeting in Cape Town at a local church. It was during a time when God was moving in a powerful way with many signs and wonders, including angelic visitations and supernatural encounters. As I was walking down the prayer line, I stopped to pray for a little girl who must have been about nine years old. As I began to pray for her, I felt the Lord say to me, "I will visit her and she will encounter my glory."

I started to prophesy over her when she stopped me and with typical childlikeness said, "Uncle Julian, I know God will visit with me because He has already taken me into heaven a few times. I have an angel come to me and usher me into God's presence and then we walk and talk together. He once took me into a body part room where I go to fetch body parts when people need healing." This young girl then began to prophesy the secrets of my heart to me as the power of God pulsated through her. It was experiential and life-changing! God had shown this little girl how to heal the sick by the Holy Spirit!

3
The Language
Of Heaven

But, as it is written, "What no eye has seen, nor ear heard, nor the heart of man imagined, what God has prepared for those who love Him"— these things God has revealed to us through the Spirit. For the Spirit searches everything, even the depths of God. 1 Corinthians 2:9-12

God wants to develop a relationship with you that opens up the very depths of His heart to you. He wants to speak to you and develop your own love language with Him. Here are some prophetic experiences and types of revelation to help you. This is not exhaustive, but I believe it will help you understand some ways in which God will interact with His people. Revelation can be and is often expressed in the following ways:

Impressions

These are moments when we "sense" or just "know" things in the Spirit. Jesus had an encounter where He received knowledge by the Spirit. The word used is "perceived". In Luke 5:22 the Bible says that Jesus "perceived" in the Spirit that they were reasoning amongst themselves. That word "perceived" is sometimes translated as "knowing" (Matthew 9:4). The Greek word speaks of an ability to know fully and to be acquainted in a discerning, recognising manner. Most times when I flow in a word of knowledge, it starts out with a "knowing" or a "sensing" of a need. This can manifest in a sympathetic pain in my body or by simply having a strong impression in my heart. Often I can walk into a situation and sense a specific need that is to be met by God and I bring directive prayer and faith for it to be done.

The Voices of God

Let's look at the audible voice of God first. Paul, on the road to Damascus, had an encounter with God where people actually heard the voice of Jesus with their natural ears but saw no one (Acts 9:7). Although, as of yet, I have not heard the audible voice of God, many have testified to hearing it with their natural ears.

The second way God speaks (and this is in no order of importance) is through what is called an internal audible voice.

I have heard this a few times in my life and it is a clear and distinct voice that I hear inside my being. It is clearly different from my own thoughts or impressions and it catches my attention immediately. I first heard this when I was 15 when I heard God call me to the prophetic ministry. It was clear. He said, "I will raise you up as a prophet to the nations."

I remember being in my room when that happened. As I walked out of my room, a family friend who had a prophetic gift looked at me and began to prophesy. She said that she'd had a dream the previous night where the Lord spoke to her about me being a prophet who would reveal the secrets of people's hearts.

Then there is the most frequently experienced voice, which is the still, small voice of the Holy Spirit. Elijah heard this when he asked God to speak to him (1 Kings 19:11-13). This can come in a variety of ways and is most often the way God speaks to me. I lean into God as He speaks, very often clearly and directly. Thoughts, which are clearly not my own pop into my head and a message is revealed to me. Words of knowledge are most often received in this way. There is a wonderful peace and easy flow that comes with these words.

Trances

The most notable account of a trance is recorded in Acts when Peter experiences a trance (Acts 10:10). This is a very interesting encounter and forms the basis for the breaking out of salvation amongst the gentiles. Please note that the gospel coming to us as part of the gentile nations was as a result of a revelatory experience. Many people seem to be afraid of this word "trance" as it sounds like it is from the new age. But it is a biblical word and we are not to be afraid of it.

The Greek word for "trance" is closely associated with the word "ecstasy". It speaks of replacing your ordinary state of mind with an elevated, God-given state in order to receive prophetic revelation. As I said earlier in this book, I have had one encounter where it felt as if I were suspended in time as God began to speak to me about a new shape of prophetic ministry. It felt like time stood still and God began to speak to me about not domesticating the prophetic ministry. I was clearly involved in the experience and at times I felt physically what was happening. When I came out of the trance, I felt encouraged and strengthened.

Visions

There are different types of visions listed in the Bible. I will try and briefly explain them to you.

An *open eye* vision is when we see clearly with our eyes in the physical (Paul had such a vision. See Acts 16:8-10. There are many such encounters listed in the Bible). This has not happened to me often, but I was once in an area in South Africa called Clarens when the Lord opened my eyes to physically see the host of heavenly angels around the mountains. It was amazing! The bright light shining from them was startling!

Sometimes it seems as if something is superimposed over the natural. This often happens when I see angels or when I am involved in bringing deliverance and I see the demon walk in with the person.

A *moving vision* is like a movie that is being shown to us as we encounter God. I often get these as I prophesy over people. You will hear me say, "I see you…" in my prophetic flow. This is because I am actually seeing something above or around the person and I declare what I am seeing.

Often, as I am describing a room or an encounter someone might have had, it will be like a movie and there will be details that I will recount from that. Ezekiel received revelation in the form of visions from God when he received his prophetic encounter (see Ezekiel 1). He was seeing something moving and taking shape as he prophesied.

Another type of vision is the *inner open vision*. This is when our eyes are open yet we see the picture in our mind. Many people receive this kind of visionary experience but do not recognize it as coming from God, because they have not understood it as being more than just their imagination. This speaks of the eyes of our heart (Ephesians 1:18). The word "heart" is sometimes translated as "understanding" or "mind". In other words, the eyes of our mind are seeing something that we are to comprehend.

Finally, a *closed vision* is when our eyes are closed and we receive revelation.

I have had powerful encounters with God when I have had these pictorial and symbolic visions. They have helped shape and prepare me for what God wants. I had an encounter with God where He walked me through a stadium, telling me about some of the nations I would go to and minister in. A number of them came to pass some months after receiving the vision.

Open Heaven Encounters

The Bible often records experiences where people talk about an open heaven. This simply refers to a spiritual encounter with God where there is an uninterrupted interaction between heaven and earth. Jacob's ladder is one such example, where we see angels ascending and descending from heaven to earth (Genesis 28).

There are doors or openings in the Spirit that will open us up to the purposes of God. They act as transition points between the supernatural and the natural.

This is different from walking under an open heaven in the general sense. I believe this is what happened for Isaiah, Ezekiel and John as they encountered Him. This is an actual engaging in the heavenly realm. A number of times in meetings I have seen the heavens open (like a portal opening in the roof, with heaven's light breaking in), which helps me see what God is doing. At times it will seem physical and often it will be manifested in a dramatic breakout of powerful manifestations, like gold dust, oil, or even whirlwinds. I find that during these times things seem to be clear and the sense of the dynamic power of God is present in an amazing way. Unusual miracles often happen in this context!

Lift up your heads, O you gates! And be lifted up, you everlasting doors! And the King of glory shall come in. Psalm 24:7

He commanded the clouds above and opened the doors of *Heaven.* Psalm 78:23

Most assuredly, I say to you, hereafter you shall see Heaven open, and the angels of God ascending and descending upon the Son of Man. John 1:51

After these things I looked, and behold, a door standing open in Heaven. And the first voice which I heard was like a trumpet speaking with me, saying "Come up here, and I will show you things which must take place after this. Immediately, I was in the spirit. Revelation 4:1-2a

Dreams

Many people forget that often God speaks to us in dreams. Joseph is a prime example of a man who had dreams that directed his future (Genesis 37).

There is a lot for us to study and learn in the area of dreams. I want to recommend a book by Jim Goll called *Dream Language*. On a number of occasions I have had dreams that have helped me to discern the will of God in a particular situation or when there is a need to intercede. A dream I had one particular night had to do with my grandmother. I woke from a dream where my gran was incredibly ill and looked as if she was dying. In my dream I saw exactly what was happening and when I woke up I began to pray fervently for her. I phoned my mom the next day and described to her what I saw. It was just as I had dreamed. I believe it was a key for me to pray and ask God for her life!

Angelic Visitations

This is a subject all by itself. An angelic visitation is a biblical experience and we should not be afraid of it. The early church seemed to have regular encounters with angels. As we saw earlier, when Peter was released from prison by an angelic visitation and knocked on the door where they were praying for him, they simply insisted *"...it is only his angel"* (Acts 12:15). It seemed that they were very open to angelic visitations and even expected them!

In an encounter I had in France, the Lord opened my eyes to an angel that was positioned behind the drummer (although we don't always see them physically, as in the case of Cornelius who saw an angel in a vision in Acts 10:3).

A great sense of fear and excitement came over me as I began to prophesy and share what I was seeing. It was the most beautiful thing I have seen. His tunic was the most amazing translucent gold and he had the most incredible pair of shoes on his feet. The sword in his hand was huge and stretched across the length of the room. These were important images as I felt the Lord say this was an angel sent to commission the French people for battle. God moved powerfully that night and many people encountered God, along with the powerful deliverance of a young man. Others testified to seeing angels later that week too.

There are a number of other supernatural encounters in the Bible that I will mention briefly: supernatural transportation (1 Kings18: 11-12), being translated in the Spirit (2 Corinthians

12:2-4), and experiences in the heavens (Exodus 24:9-11). All of these must point to Jesus and His church. The aim of these experiences is to build up the church and not for spiritual bravado. That is why God gives them. They help establish the church in its mandate to reach the world. That's the point of it all!

The Gifts of the Holy Spirit

Before anyone can begin to understand spiritual gifts we have to understand that if we are not motivated by love we should give up trying right now. Also, we make mistakes and we are never always going to get it right. That's okay! God uses that to His glory anyway.

1 Corinthians 12:1 says, *"Now concerning spiritual gifts, brethren, I do not want you to be ignorant…"* Here Paul gives us clear apostolic direction concerning the gifts of the Holy Spirit. Continuing in the same chapter he begins to talk about the body of Christ and how it functions and fits together (v12-31). He then continues in chapter 13 speaking about how in everything we must be motivated by love.

Then in chapter 14 he picks up the same theme concerning the gifts of the Holy Spirit in an even stronger way. He starts off by saying, *"Pursue love, and desire spiritual gifts."* "Desire" means to be zealous for or to burn with desire for the gifts. Negatively it means to be jealous for the gifts. Those are strong words from Paul. Why does he want us to desire the gifts so much?

I believe the key is this: the gifts of the Holy Spirit are given to us to help build up and encourage the church of Jesus Christ (1 Corinthians 14:12). They are also a sign that there is activity or manifestations of the Holy Spirit's presence to the church and the unbeliever (1 Corinthians 12:4; 14: 24).

Faith levels are raised when there are displays of the gifts of the Holy Spirit in the church. When we allow the Holy Spirit to manifest Himself in His gifts to the church we are helping to prepare the bride of Christ on her way to perfection.

There are nine gifts that the Holy Spirit graces us with. They are different from other spiritual gifts in that the Holy Spirit gives them to us as they are needed.

Although people can operate in a particular gift regularly (i.e. prophecy), these are given as the situation arises. You can find them in 1 Corinthians 12:1-10. We will look at them in groups of three.

REVELATION GIFTS

These are gifts that reveal something concerning a person or a situation.

Word of Wisdom: This is a supernatural ability to know God's heart concerning a situation in the future and how to deal with it. It gives divine means as to how to accomplish God's will in a situation.

Word of Knowledge: This is the ability to know something about a person or situation that has been revealed supernaturally by God.

Gifts of Discerning of Spirits: This is the ability to discern what spiritual beings (angels or demons) are in operation in a person or situation.

POWER GIFTS

These are gifts that demonstrate the power of God in operation.

The Gift of Faith: This is a supernatural faith to believe God for the impossible to take place in a person's life or situation.

The Gift of Working Miracles: This is the ability to release the supernatural in the natural. This is when God performs an act that cannot be done by man. It is power to counteract earthly and evil forces.

Gifts of Healings: This is when there is a supernatural healing without human aid (doctors, etc.).

VOCAL GIFTS

These are gifts that speak out what is on God's heart.

The Gift of Tongues: This is a divinely inspired ability to speak forth in a tongue/unknown language publicly. It is always accompanied by an interpretation.

Interpretation of Tongues: This is when an inspired message in tongues is interpreted in a known language.

Prophecy: This is a divinely inspired utterance and it comes to reveal the heart of God. It is often the gift that is used as a vehicle for all the other gifts. It is to simply hear God and to speak out what is on His heart.

Any believer can use the gifts of the Holy Spirit, BUT it will be nothing but a load of clanging cymbals if it is not accompanied by love (1 Corinthians 13). The gifts are never ours to possess. They are the Holy Spirit's. We are simply like postmen, delivering a letter to His people. In order for any gift to be just that, it must be shared. It only becomes a gift when it is given to somebody else. The gift is never for you to hold onto; it is for you to give to someone else.

4
Wisdom
And Revelation

I do not cease to give thanks for you, remembering you in my prayers, that the God of our Lord Jesus Christ, the Father of glory, may give you a spirit of wisdom and of revelation in the knowledge of Him, having the eyes of your hearts enlightened, that you may know what is the hope to which He has called you, what are the riches of His glorious inheritance in the saints, and what is the immeasurable greatness of His power toward us who believe, according to the working of His great might.
Ephesians 1:16-18

Revelation must always be coupled with wisdom. Often the Bible connects wisdom and revelation together (Ephesians 1:17).

The Greek word for wisdom speaks of an ability to rightly apply revelation. Paul speaks of this wisdom when he refers to the mystery of Jesus that is now revealed to us by the Spirit (1 Corinthians 2:7-13).

It is very clear that this is not a wisdom that comes from man. It has to be compared by taking that which is spiritual and comparing it with spiritual things! It is not a carnal or human-inspired wisdom. This wisdom comes by the administration of the Holy Spirit. It requires faith for us to enter into it. If we are to come into an ever-increasing flow of revelation, we must make sure that our basis of revelation is found in the scriptures.

Many prophetic ministries who flow in revelation have been shut down because they have failed to understand their experiences though a biblical filter.

The new age movement has now counterfeited prophetic encounters and as a result I find that we are wary of anything that cannot be measured by a cerebral or rational mindset. In the encounter with Moses and the Egyptian magicians, we see that both Moses and the Egyptians performed the same miracles. It was Moses' staff ultimately that had authority over the demonic forces of Egypt (Exodus 7:8-13).

The battle for the supernatural involves understanding origin or source. The Egyptians could counterfeit all that Moses did, yet it was Aaron's rod that swallowed up the rest.

They could only counterfeit what Moses did and their source was demonic rather than from the Spirit of God.

I was in a meeting in England once when a newly saved lady *Pyschic* came up to me and told me that she had been a clairvoyant. She *witch* then told me how accurate she had been and how she could tell the secrets of people's hearts in the same way as I was doing through the prophetic ministry. She was very confused about why she was seeing such accurate ministry in the church!

Her only reference for power was the demonic. I explained to her that all she had been involved in was a counterfeit. I then asked her a few questions about her experiences. Underlying it all was an uncontrollable force that made her lose her temper every day. Even in her attempt to use her gift for good, she had no control over it. She was plugged into the wrong source! I prayed for her to be filled with the Holy Spirit and to begin to operate in genuine prophetic ministry.

Rightly applying what God gives to the church is as important as receiving His gifts. We must be wise in both receiving the prophetic revelation and stepping out in the prophetic. All prophetic encounters and revelation should always point to Jesus. Anything that does not point to Him is empty at best and demonic at worst. He is the central figure of all prophecy. In fact it is the testimony of Jesus that is the spirit of prophecy (Revelation 19:10). I must underline how important it is to apply wisdom to all we do.

Many prophetic ministries prophesy out of an incorrect understanding of two things: firstly the authority of the Bible and secondly, the connection between prophetic revelation and apostolic application.

If we do not put these two values high on our agenda, we will be open to false doctrine, which in turn will affect the way we live. For example, I have heard prophets prophesy that particular individuals would get married because God had put them aside for each other.

This comes from a theology that removes the choice of the believer in the choosing of a marriage partner. The implications of this theology give rise to many other questions which will eventually lead to a mess: what happens if I married the wrong person? Can I now get divorced? Or what if I only married the person I am with in response to a prophetic word, yet I do not get along with them or worse still, I do not love them?

Can you see how easy it becomes to miss out on God's revealed will in the Bible and derail our destiny because of an incorrect prophecy? I have seen this operate in some churches too. Some have received a prophetic word about a new "revelation" that is extra-biblical. The result is deception. This does no favours for prophetic ministries.

In Acts 11 we see the prophet Agabus bring a prophetic word that there will be a drought. The disciples respond in faith, for though they had not yet seen the evidence of the drought they

took a collection for the churches who would be in need. T
a very interesting response and teaches us a few things about
applying wisdom to prophetic revelation.

It seems to me that the prophets travelled together. In the Acts
13 account of this predictive prophecy it makes mention that
there were prophets who came down from Jerusalem. These
were men recognised for their prophetic ministry.

For some elders and leaders in local churches it has been a
difficult thing to recognize and release emerging prophetic
voices in their churches. Yet it is vitally important to release
these gifts in the church in order to build up and restore her to
all she should be.

As an aside, I want to give some practical wisdom as to how
one should raise up and release prophetic people in the church.
The following is not exhaustive or prescriptive in anyway. These
are simply some pointers that I have picked up through my
experiences.

I am sure a large part of this might seem subjective and "touchy-
feely", but that's the nature of the prophetic! So here are some
keys to recognising prophetically gifted people:

A strong sense of calling to the prophetic. Whilst the prophetic
should be desired and longed for in every believer's life (1
Corinthians 14:1), a prophetic person will live with a sense of
calling from God to minister, flow in and sense the heart of God

in a way that is not ordinary. Often, emerging prophetic gifts will testify to growing up with a sense of knowing things, a sense of having "inside information" and a unique ability to really empathize and sense others' deep feelings.

Often thoughts will be popping into their minds as words of knowledge are released without them even having to ask for them! It's as if God has put His hand on such people without their permission. They will often feel things that they cannot articulate, but will just "know" that what they sense is true and will happen.

You will often find that **prophetic people have lived through seasons of extreme rejection**. This might not be true for everyone, but it is my experience that prophetic people will often go through hardships and rejection that will drive them into deeper intimacy with God. This is often why prophetic people are misunderstood to be shy, introverted and seriously insecure!

The reason I put this in here is that very seldom do you find a confident prophet. Most prophetic people will live with a sense of insecurity and a lack of confidence. You will see this clearly as you watch the life of an emerging prophetic person.

Prophetic people will often seem to have "foot-in-mouth" disease. They will often say things without realising what they are saying and will put their foot in it. They can touch on something that has been an issue and then pass their opinion (or sometimes God's wisdom) on it without even realising it. Sometimes it will seem as if they come across as intense and very black and white. This is not to be misunderstood as sharpness or being too direct, it just seems to be the way prophets work.

 The most obvious clue to being prophetic is prophecy. I am not simply talking about bringing low-level words. These words must carry a sense of God's direction, a sense of revelation that is previously unknown and a weightiness that moves the church on in God. Just because one brings contributions regularly in a meeting does not make you prophetic! Anyone can operate in the gift of prophecy. But there is a lifestyle that is attached to prophetic people that will set them apart from the gift of prophecy. They are the gift. It's not that they simply have a gift; it is that they *are* the gift. Who they are is the package you have to receive if you want a prophet in your midst.

Being responsive

I also notice in the Acts 11 encounter that the churches respond in faith immediately. Most people wait in a place of apathy hoping that the word will come to pass. Only in retrospect, when the word has happened, do they act on it. The church in Antioch responded immediately. They determined in their hearts to bless the churches in Judea and made provision for Barnabas and Saul to carry the money (see Acts 11:27-30).

Prophecy is always connected to faith. It is not fatalism. Either we can receive the word and act in faith upon it, or we can miss what God wants to do! The application of this is connected to wisdom. We must note a few things before we just jump into a word. These prophets seem to have a track record with the disciples. They are recognised by both the church and other apostles.

In fact, they seemed to carry enough spiritual weight that they could ordain and release people into ministry (Acts 13). It is because of this recognition that I believe the disciples could respond with wisdom and bring some application to the word.

There was also a sense of witness where everyone according to their own ability gave into the offering.

It speaks of a corporate witness to the value of the word. We have to make sure that, when a word comes with predictive revelation, leadership weighs it and if it seems right, we act upon it. In 1 Corinthians 14 we see that the church together is meant to weigh the word and respond to its conditions. To not do this is to devalue prophecy and treat it with contempt.

Another aspect to discerning the revelation one receives and applying wisdom to it comes in the context of prayer. In the story of Elijah we see him bring a word to the nation of Israel about a drought.

It seems to me that God likes to make a points through droughts. To grab the attention of evil Ahab and the people of Israel He sends a drought (1 Kings 17). For three years, at the word of Elijah, there is no rain whatsoever. There is no precipitation.

Nothing. The book of James seems to give us a hint as to how this came about.

Sometimes we think that when something has been prophesied, we no longer have any more responsibility. That is not true. In James 5:17 we see the key to this word coming to pass:

Elijah was a man with a nature like ours, and he prayed fervently that it might not rain, and for three years and six months it did not rain on the earth. Then he prayed again, and heaven gave rain, and the earth bore its fruit.

Do you see the subtle difference between prophecy and prayer? Elijah prayed and it sustained the word he prophesied. That is one of the most amazing lessons to be learned in the prophetic. Prayer. It is the effective collaboration of heaven and earth! If we want to apply revelation from God correctly, it must be bathed in prayer. It is the sustaining factor in prophecy.

Lastly, I want to mention the working together of apostles and prophets. As has been said earlier, I believe churches should be built on prophetic revelation that is coupled with apostolic wisdom. This should be the foundation of New Testament church life (Ephesians 2:20).

It was in Cape Town when I first experienced working with an apostle. It was with a well-missed friend and father in the faith, the late Simon Pettit. Simon and Lindsay Pettit moved to South Africa in response to the call of God in the late eighties

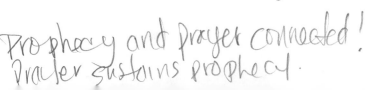
Prophecy and prayer connected! Prayer sustains prophecy.

and immediately began pioneering a new way of doing church in Cape Town. For many people who were Christians in the days during apartheid, the thought of a multi-ethnic, multi-racial church was foreign. In fact the church, which should have been a prophetic picture of all nations together, was most divided on a Sunday morning.

I don't think many churches had even thought through the apostolic doctrine or its implications of "one new man in Christ ". Simon began to model this and build the church he was serving as a community of people from different races and socio-economic backgrounds, releasing them into places of influence and leadership together as a family. This was pretty much unheard of. At the time, I also belonged to a church for a number of years that had no people of colour other than my family.

Having been involved for a while in *Newfrontiers*, I had the opportunity to travel with Simon to Australia and New Zealand. I noticed that Simon highly valued the prophetic revelation I was bringing and made some major apostolic decisions based on what I had brought.

I also noticed a sharp accuracy to the words I was bringing. The most important change that happened was that I had started to catch a glimpse of a building ministry. I had been dreaming of having my own itinerant ministry before then. I was looking forward to traveling the world bringing words to people and developing a fantastic ministry.

I saw something different whilst on that trip. I saw the church that Jesus saw. It was a mystery that began to be unfolded to me. It is still unfolding to me to be honest. I saw the church being all she could be. I saw a glorious bride – a marvellous display of the wisdom of God.

I can never underestimate the effect of that trip on my life. I finally saw the price Jesus paid for the church – the price He paid for local churches all over the world.

And this is why we need to build with the revelation God gives us. Simon painted a picture for me that displayed the church as a representation of the resurrected, glorious Jesus. She was radiant and showing forth the kingdom of God in a radical way. When prophetic ministers see this, their prophesying takes on the shape of holy expectation rather than earthbound negativity. One begins to fly when you fall in love with Jesus and His church.

Since then I have had the privilege of working in two apostolic teams building into France and the north of England. This has meant working with apostolic men who have taken revelation I have received about church plants, new leaders, new ministries and many other aspects of church life, and have applied it to various situations – and the result has been amazing fruit.

We have seen buildings bought, people moving localities and miracles released, as men and women have responded in faith to the prophetic word.

Revelation and wisdom go together. Paul reminds us, though, that we must first have the eyes of our heart opened in order to see what He wants to do. Our hearts must be open and ready to receive if we want the full weight of the prophetic released in our churches and in our lives.

Prayer a Prophecy
Revelation a Wisdom

5
Positioned
For Revelation

Having gifts that differ according to the grace given to us, let us use them: if prophecy, in proportion to our faith...
Romans 12:6

I once heard somebody say, "Your expectation is God's invitation." I like that. Most people miss out on receiving powerful revelation from God because they simply do not expect it. If we are to receive revelation from the Father, we have to be a people of faith. Most teaching that comes from the "word of faith" movement places an emphasis on the legal right of the believer to "claim" certain truths in the Bible. The result is a reward without any value on relationship. But this is a distortion of true, biblical faith.

As a young boy I had various illnesses and frequently struggled with my health. I would often wake up in the middle of the night with severe ear pain and instinctively cry out for my father to come to my aid.

The truth is, I had every right as his child to demand that he come and help me. Yet this was not my motivation. It was his tenderness and touch that soothed me more than my rights as a child.

His duty towards me was motivated by his love for me as his son. My response to him was complete confidence. I knew that he would come to me the minute I called out his name. This was because I knew he loved me. I had faith in his ability to help me because of my confidence in his love for me. This is the connecting factor of faith!

Faith is not something many evangelicals talk about any more. We place a high emphasis on a correct understanding of the word of God, yet for most it does not produce powerful living. The result of correct understanding should be correct living. We often place value on a cerebral understanding rather than faith-filled revelation (yet none of the gifts work without faith.)

The Bible says that correct understanding is first found in faith. It is by faith we understand that the universe was created (Hebrews 11:3). This principle laid down by the writer to the Hebrews is so important. Most westerners are afraid to step out in truth because they do not fully comprehend everything.

Yet faith sets its sights on that which is unseen and manifests itself in obedience.

One just needs to read casually through the Bible to see that every person who did anything significant for God had to step into the realm of the unknown in order to see the full outworking of God's purposes. If we are to receive revelation, the depth and shape of that revelation is in direct proportion to our faith.

The implications of this truth are mind-blowing! It means that Enoch, Abraham, Moses, David and many other men and women of God received the revelation of who God is because they chose to receive it by faith.

Think about Abraham, who against the backdrop of sun gods, moon gods and all the other gods that were around in his day, encoun-tered Yahweh, the true God. He responded in faith by obeying Yahweh and moving his whole family to a place called "there"! It was this faith that produced in him a righteous standing with God.

Faith takes that which is unseen and manifests it through a radical obedience – and it is through this process that we then receive understanding as to the nature and character of God. He is a rewarder of those who diligently seek Him. Faith is active.

I could tell you story after story of God's faithfulness to me simply because I obeyed his leading by faith. One of the key areas of obedience and faith I learnt as a young, ambitious man who wanted to travel the world and serve God's purposes. I knew I had a call on my life and back then the way you walked into the fulfillment of your calling was to go to Bible school. A good Bible school meant going to America, so when I left school, I got a scholarship to a prominent prophetic school in Kansas City, USA.

However, I felt God call me to serve my local church at the time and forfeit the adventure of travel. I remember feeling depressed at the thought of not being able to live out my dream. God promised that I would travel when the time was right, if I was faithful to serve in the hidden place. If I did that He would give me a platform in the public place. It took another 6 years before I was suddenly thrust onto the international scene and saw my destiny begin unfolding. I have now travelled to over 20 nations!

To live apart from faith is to default the pleasure of God on your life. God is pleased with faith (Hebrews 11:6). Jesus often rebuked His disciples for their lack of faith, even after they had seen a demonstration of God's power.

One would think that if you had seen miracles over weather patterns, many sick people being healed, food multiplication or even the dead being raised, you would have faith. Not so for Jesus' disciples!

Even though they had seen many miracles they still had to overcome a few hurdles in order to get a full revelation of how to live by faith. In Matthew 16:8-12 Jesus rebukes the disciples

for their lack of faith because they could not discern what h
was teaching them concerning the impact of the Pharisees and
Sadducees.

There are some clear lessons to be learned here. As Jesus begins
to talk about leaven, the disciples naturally think He is referring
to something physical and temporal. They immediately set their
attention on a felt need.

Most of us live like this. We are predisposed to the realm of the
natural. Jesus rebukes them for not realizing that He is talking
about the unseen reality of God's kingdom. They are thinking
about physical food when Jesus wants to reveal a spiritual reality.

This is also shown in the difference between Jacob and Esau.
Esau gave up his inheritance to satisfy a temporary need. He
gave up something of lasting value for a need that would be
satisfied in a moment.

Many Christians do this. They give up an eternal inheritance
for a temporary fix. Esau was rejected by God because of this
(Hebrews 12:17). All because of a single meal – something
tangible that cost him his unseen inheritance.

Jesus rebuked the disciples because their orientation. Their
natural default was to evaluate spiritual things by earthly
criteria. Jesus could easily have provided bread miraculously. All
He needed to do was ask His father. It was only then that they
understood He was talking about the teaching of the Pharisees.

The Pharisees placed emphasis on an external obedience to the law without any change in their hearts. It was all about what happened on the outside. It required no faith to observe the law externally. Jesus said of the Pharisees that they did not even believe in the law of Moses. If they did, they would have recognized Jesus as the Messiah. The very scriptures pointed to Him (John 5:40-47).

The Pharisees did not read the law with faith, looking forward to the hope of the promised Messiah. As a result they missed the heart of the law. They didn't understand that it pointed to Jesus who is the fulfillment of the law!

Anyone who responds to God with a lack of faith will be affected by the leaven of the Pharisees, which eventually affects everything and taints it with unbelief and sin. Your life simply becomes one of works and striving in order to obey religious laws rather than one of faith which responds to grace-filled revelation.

Faith sets as its target the unseen realities of the kingdom. It is the evidence of that which is unseen. As we respond to truth and revelation, they will unlock ever-increasing faith.

Jesus likens the design of faith to a mustard seed (Matthew 17:20). He is simply illustrating that this little seed grows to become a big tree. Here's the point: faith must be growing in order to be effective. Too many believers live at the level of saving faith and never grow into prevailing faith. Faith that keeps you in the midst of a trial, faith that releases confidence in prayer and faith that shapes the way you prophesy, must come out of increased revelation of who Jesus is.

When I started out in the prophetic, I had been touched by the love of God in an incredible way. Most of my words carried with them an emphasis on the love of God. I found out that as I had experienced the love of God and had begun to have a peek into the glorious power of God's love, I could prophesy with authority and confidence to those who were broken and rejected.

My faith was stirred because of revelation and so I could prophesy with clarity, direction and power into the lives of the broken. This is also true of healing. Only once I had received revelation that the nature of God is expressed in healing did I get to see more healings! God is a healer. That is His name after all: Yahweh is my healer. Once I had seen that in His word and experienced it as I prayed for the sick, faith rose in my heart to proclaim healing over illnesses.

I have faith, not in my ability to believe, but in my complete confidence that Yahweh is my healer! My prophesying has come out of an experiential revelation of the resurrected Christ. Faith now sets the tone for the prophetic in my life – faith to see clearly the word of the Lord and faith to enjoy the fulfilment of that word.

Safeguarding Against Deception

In the book *The Beginner's Guide to the Gift of Prophecy* by Dr.

Jack Deere, he lists ten rules for prophetic success:

"If we obey the following ten rules we may avoid some unnecessary trouble. Rule One: emphasize the main and the plain, not the rare and the bizarre. Do this in your Scripture study and in your prophetic ministry. Rule Two: don't do anything strange without a clear leading from God. Rule Three: don't do anything prophetically that is potentially embarrassing or harmful to another person without his or her permission. If you object, 'Elijah and Elisha did not have to get permission before they did harmful things,' remember, they were prophesying against God's enemies. You are ministering to his children. That is a big difference."

"Also remember that you are not Elijah or Elisha. When you get to their level of commitment and skill, you can have a little more latitude with rule three. Rule Four: repeat after me, 'I am not an exception to the rules. I am a beginner in the school of the prophets.' Rules Five through Ten: the same as Rule Four. Strive to be as normal and unreligious as possible if you want your message to be received."

Judging and Weighing Up Prophecy

Under the old covenant, prophets were stoned to death for presumptuous words. Thank God that does not happen any more. However, in the church we still seem to have a similar attitude. We think that if someone makes a mistake, he or she is not from God.

This is not true. 1 Corinthians 13:9 tells us that we know in p
therefore we prophesy in part. The prophets of old spoke the
very words of God (2 Peter 1:20-21). We now are beholding God
and do not have a full revelation of Him yet (2 Corinthians 3:18).
That is why we very often make mistakes. The keys for judging
prophetic words are simple.

- Are they soundly based on God's Word?
- Do they bring glory to God or the speaker?
- Does the word edify, exhort and comfort (1 Corinthians 14:3)?
- Are there signs of manipulation and control?
- Is it super-spiritual? e.g. "God told me to tell you..."
- Does it bring confirmation?
- Is the word coming to pass?
- Does the level of prophecy match up with the person's character? e.g. God does not often give a directive word to a novice in the prophetic ministry.
- Is the word consistent with the character of God as revealed in the scripture?

Growing in Your Prophetic Gift

Our gift will only go as far as our character allows. Our character
is as important as our gift. Paul's cry was never about gifting, it
was about getting to know and become more like Jesus.

Without the character of God being displayed in our life, the
words we give will have no weight or depth to them. God wants
us to reflect Him in our character.

Hang out with other prophetic people. They will spur you on. Something seems to happen when prophetic people get together. We will grow with each other as we ask questions and stir one another for more of God.

The good news is that prophetic people often live in what is coming tomorrow; the bad news is that people do not understand that today. So it is good to be with people from time to time who understand each other, rather than becoming frustrated because things are not going our way.

Develop a passionate prayer life. Not all intercessors are prophetic but all prophetic people are intercessors. We get to know the heart of God as we pray and feel His affection about issues. Be known as a prayer warrior. Be known as someone who is found in the scriptures. Make sure that you are devouring the Bible like your "daily bread"! The Word of God is our highest authority. It is more valuable than prophecy! If you get to know it, your prophetic gift will become sharpened.

Stay humble. God opposes the proud and gives grace to the humble (James 4:6). The gift of prophecy is a grace gift. If you want more of it, keep humble. Do not get puffed up. If your heart is full of pride God will not take delight in you. You will get words, but you will drive people away and never show His heart to others.

Get involved in a local church. Ephesians 3:10-11 tells us that the eternal purpose of God is expressed in His church. The gifts of God are to edify the church and this can only be done if you are a committed and functioning member of a church. Itinerant ministries have their place, but they do not practically help build in a local church.

If you want to make a real difference in the prophetic ministry it must come out of relationship. Get stuck in and serve with your gift. Not only will you have the necessary leadership to help guide you, but you will also release the grace given to you for the body of Christ (Ephesians 4:15; 16). Jesus is coming back for His church and not for a ministry.

Recognising False Prophets

I would like to share some thoughts on prophetic ministry and how we should relate to it in the midst of some very confusing prophetic models. Part of this means we will have to deal with false prophets. Recognising a false prophet is becoming more important as the day of Christ's return draws near. The devil will always attempt to counterfeit what God is doing so that he can deceive God's people.

Jude 4-19 gives a good description of the false ones who would try to deceive the people of God. Here are some others:

- They will deny the deity of Jesus.
- They will deny the authority of God's word.
- Their lives will not be consistent with their message.
- There will be identifiable sin that they won't repent of.
- They will gather people to themselves before they reveal

their true selves and thus deceive even the elect if possible.

- There will be no fruit of the Holy Spirit evident in their lives.
- Glory that is due to Jesus will be shifted to themselves or the devil.

Never be moved by miracles and power. Jesus promises us that there will be those with power to do miracles that are false prophets. Power is never meant to be the defining factor of whether something is from God or not. When Moses had his show down with Pharaoh's magicians (Exodus 7) we see that the magicians could do all the same miracles that Aaron's staff did. The difference was the source! Aaron's rod had the final authority because Aaron and Moses were plugged into the right source! Look for the fruits that point to Jesus.

When God Goes Silent

Another aspect to prophetic ministry is during the season when God goes silent. Part of the prophetic ministry is about seeking after God. Often heaven will go silent on us and we will have to press into God without sensing His presence and anointing. This is often a difficult time and can cause a prophetic person much frustration. However, see this as an opportunity to learn more about God and you will see it work out for your good.

I often play hide-and-seek with my niece. I love the look on her face when she finds me. Her face lights up with excitement and absolute joy! I hide myself in a place where I know she can find me. All the fun would be taken out if I left home and she never found me. It's the same with God. He hides Himself for us, not

*God hides himself for us, not from us. His heart lights up with Joy when He sees us get excited about finding him

from us. His heart lights up with joy when He sees us get excited about finding Him. I know it's difficult when you're in the midst of a difficult situation and can't hear from God. But keep focused on what you know to be true about God. Keep worshipping Him. Keep seeking after Him. You will be found by Him!

Live the Life

I want to conclude by encouraging you that this life is not just about words. It is about living a prophetic life. It costs you to live a life of prophetic significance.

I felt the Lord once give an impression of my life being like a signpost on a dusty road at night. It was just stuck out in the middle of nowhere. The only time something happened was when headlights shone on it and people were able to see which way to go. That is true of anyone with a prophetic ministry. It can get lonely and sometimes even dark.

When God chooses to shine on us we point the way for His people to go. When we are in His presence and He shines His light on us, nothing can compare to the glorious sense of His purpose for us.

Sharing His heart with others and seeing lives changed because of the prophetic word is more than worth it. The cost is nothing compared to the price Jesus paid for me to hear His voice. In light of the joy and pleasure I get out of being a friend of God, I would not change any of the difficult circumstances I have had to go through in my life. Nothing compares to knowing Him!

What then, brothers? When you come together, each one has a hymn, a lesson, a revelation, a tongue, or an interpretation. Let all things be done for building up. 1 Corinthians 14:26

In conclusion I want to quote Dr Martyn Lloyd-Jones preaching on this text in Westminster Chapel, London, in November 1959.

"We have so far departed from the kind of thing Paul is speaking about here that the Church, speaking generally, is as she is at the present time. Let me therefore put it like this. What is the setting here? It is a typical picture of the early Church with men and women 'filled with Spirit.' The Apostle is not giving them an account of what should happen in formal service such as we normally have today, or such as you may have in a cathedral. You are in an entirely different realm. I see very little in common between what the Apostle describes and what we are so familiar with. No, the whole thing is different. Let us remember that the contrast in his mind is that old type of jollification under the influence of drink. The kind of service, the kind of meeting Paul is describing is something which has got, at any rate, something of that element in it. There is joy, there is freedom, there is happiness, there is inspiration; and we must not shut that out."

He goes on to say "...that then is the sort of thing that you and I have got to bear in mind as we try to understand this particular statement. Here is a gathering of men and women who are filled with the Spirit of God, and each one of them has got something, one a psalm, one a doctrine, one revelation, one an interpretation, one a tongue. Here they are overfull with this, as it were, and wanting to say it. And as each one gave his contribution the others rejoiced and they praised God together; and they were all in a state of great joy and glory and of happiness."

Join in the festivities of heaven. Step out in boldness. You have something to give that will bless and build the church up. At the end of it all, God looks to the heart and He will use our failures and our successes to build us into all that He wants us to be.

6
Religion Sucks

During my early years of pastoring I had the privilege of ministering at many high school camps. At one of these camps, I was speaking on worship and our response to the mercy of God.

Romans 12 was my text. I emphasised the kindness of God in witholding the judgement that was our rightful due. During that time the Lord gave me a word of knowledge about a young girl who had had an abortion. Together with a lady friend I listened as a girl, who had responded to the word, poured out her heart and described the agony she had experienced in having the abortion.

It had been almost a year to that day. She shared how there was no one in her church to talk to. In fact, her having the abortion meant she had committed one of the "worst" sins. The healing community of the church only offered her condemnation and no grace.

It was good to see the power of God break in and bring the revelation that God had set her free from all condemnation.

I once had the opportunity to share the good news of God's kingdom with a couple on the brink of divorce. As a single person at the time, I had no clue about marriage. As I spoke to them over the course of a weekend I asked God for insight as to how I could help this dear couple.

I realised as I was sharing with them that although they had both attended church, the power of salvation and the truth of grace had never been an experience for them personally. They had tried various religions and attempts at getting close to Jesus but failed hopelessly. I will never forget when this dear lady said to me, "I thought grace was simply something we did before we ate!" Thankfully, at the end of the week both of them had got saved and filled with the Holy Spirit and as far as I know they are together and very happy.

Both these stories illustrate how easy it is to be a part of something that *seems* godly but is entrenched in religion. You can be part of a church that has all the right theology and practice but lacks the power of God to bring salvation and healing to the broken. Paul called it a *form* of godliness, but without its power (2 Timothy 3:5).

The greatest threat to the church of Jesus Christ is not homosexuality, pornography, abortion, satanism, the government shutting us down or even persecution. The greatest threat, I believe, is if we get caught up in a "form" of godliness and no longer listen to the voice of God.

The spirit of religion is the ugly thing that blocks the ears, eyes and sense of touch of the church and renders her ineffective and powerless.

The religious spirit seeks to replace our passion for Jesus with passion for religious activity and to take the place of the Holy Spirit in our experience of God. Jesus, addressing the religious Pharisees warned about the same thing:

O Jerusalem, Jerusalem, the city that kills the prophets and stones those who are sent to it! How often would I have gathered your children together as a hen gathers her brood under her wings, and you would not! Matthew 23:37

Prophets represented the voice of God to His people. The first thing that prophets would encounter was extreme rejection and persecution from people. Very often it would come from the "religious" leaders of the day. The religious spirit tries to crush the prophetic lifestyle.

Isaiah 55 tells us that the thoughts and ways of God are higher than our thoughts and ways. When we try to rationalise what God is saying and doing among us we are in danger of operating under the same religious spirit that the Pharisees did. God does not work according to our agenda. He does not need to consult us.

In Matthew 21 we see the triumphant entry of Jesus into Jerusalem and in verse 11 the people recognise Him as a prophet from Nazareth. They recognise Him as the voice of God in their midst. Little do they know that the coming events will speak to them in a very real and prophetic way!

Jesus goes into the temple (v12) and drives out the money-changers. After this He calls the temple of God a place of prayer. We know that prayer (communication with God) is the basis of intimacy. Jesus then begins to heal the sick and do some miracles in the temple. The people then begin to worship and praise Him, at which the Pharisees (religious ones) become indignant. The religious spirit will often try to shut down ecstatic and passionate worship because God loves to speak to us in an atmosphere of passionate worship.

The next scene is almost out of place. It's the story of the withered fig tree. God by His Holy Spirit includes this story in His word as a prophetic picture of Israel's religious system.

In the morning, as he was returning to the city, he became hungry. And seeing a fig tree by the wayside, he went to it and found nothing on it but only leaves. And he said to it, "May no fruit ever come from you again!" And the fig tree withered at once. Matthew 21:18-19

* God loves to speak in an atmosphere of passionate worship.

Jesus is hungry for fruit in the life of the c and individuals

The fig tree in this story is a signpost of the spiritual condition of many churches today. Fig trees bear fruit before they bear leaves. Jesus is hungry for fruit in the life of the church and individuals. It is interesting to note that in Genesis 3, after Adam and Eve sinned, they sewed together fig leaves as a "covering" and hid themselves from the presence of God.

In the church today, the spirit of religion has so gripped us that we have become more interested in our "coverings" – our structures, titles and being religiously correct. We are more interested in leaves than fruit. We have become caught up with saying the right things, being in the right meetings, and have effectively hidden ourselves from God's presence. But what is the use of growing in knowledge without bearing fruit?

We get so caught up in religious activity and its paraphernalia that we rely on the religious spirit to be our guide and source of revelation. The voice of God gets blocked and all we can hear is the voice of religion saying "do more ... prophesy more ... attend more meetings ... read more books ... say this and that..." etc. Before we know it, we are caught up in a system of rules and regulations that keep us from enjoying intimacy with God – and there can be no prophetic voice without intimacy.

If we are serious about living a prophetic lifestyle, then we must remain connected to God's grace and beware of being sucked into the trappings of a religious lifestyle. I offer the following checks:

Some warning signs of the religious spirit

- Inability to take correction and rebuke. Being defensive and argumentative, acting hurt and the refusal to submit to authority.
- Our prayer life becomes mechanical. We feel relief at the end of our prayer. We pray the same thing at the same time every day with no spontaneity.
- Defining the Christian life in terms of performance rather than the heart. (Discipline and will power are good, but when we take pride in what we do the religious spirit will take root in our lives).
- We begin to feel closer to God than others.
- We feel our group is on the cutting edge.
- We have a critical and judgmental spirit.
- Leadership becomes bossy, authoritative and intolerant.
- We are given to exaggeration about spiritual matters.
- We try and make physical manifestations occur in every meeting, every time. (In fact this drives away the presence of God and the power of the Spirit is nullified).

If you are thinking about how someone else should hear this teaching rather than you, then it's likely that you have a religious spirit! If God's word does not pierce your heart and affect you, it is a sign that you have a religious spirit at work in you. These are some holy cows we must kill! Although it might seem that we should not touch the so-called status quo, we have to fight the spirit of religion.

I have seen a bizzare fascination with the latest Christian gimmicks. If it's not prayer shawls from Israel or spiritual dancing as a key to breakthrough, it's following the latest 10-step teaching on "What Christians should really be eating!" (I recently heard that some Christians believe we should eat according to Old Testament law). All of this is unbiblical and not founded in a New Testament experience of grace. This kind of experience pushes us into legalistic, superstitious Christianity.

The key to overcoming the religious spirit in your life is the security of God's grace at work in you.

Ephesians 2:8 tells us that it is *"by grace that you have been saved."* It is this grace that will lead us into the good works of God that have been prepared for us to do, ever since creation. The basis of intimacy and passion for Jesus is the grace of God.

In Hebrews 4:16 we are told to *"come boldly before the throne of grace, to receive mercy and find grace in your time of need."*

If we have a clear understanding of the grace of God, our pursuit of intimacy with Him will become more passionate and this will be manifest in our prophetic gift.

But when the goodness and loving kindness of God our Savior appeared, he saved us, not because of works done by us in righteousness, but according to his own mercy, by the washing of regeneration and renewal of the Holy Spirit, whom he poured out on us richly through Jesus Christ our Savior, so that being

If we find his heart, we find his power.

justified by his grace we might become heirs according to the hope of eternal life. Titus 3:4-7

We access our promise of intimacy by the grace of God. It is not through our good works of righteousness that we have any claim to hearing His voice in the prophetic. It comes by grace. He is, therefore we can hear Him! He chooses to speak to us because He loves us. It is all by grace.

It is because of this grace that we pursue His heart in passionate worship and intimacy. If we find His heart, we find His power. The gift of prophecy is part of the _charismata_ or grace gifts. God chooses to give it to us. It's not what we do for Him that releases this gift to us. Desire, however is a prerequisite. Paul tells us in 1 Corinthians 14 to especially desire the gift of prophecy. God seems to love the pursuit of His people as they run hard after Him.

Developing passion for Jesus

"Jesus is not a doctrine, a theology, an abstract principle, a ministry, a church, a denomination, an activity, or even a way of life. Jesus is a person, a real person," says Dr Jack Deere .

Developing a passion for God cannot be taught or preached. It is an experience with Jesus. There is no easy 5-step plan to get closer to Jesus that automatically results in us feeling His presence. If you want to get to know Him you must spend time with Him! You cannot get passionate about someone you do not know. Take time to listen to Him. Be spontaneous about

Take time to listen to Jesus. Be Spontaneou spending time with him.

Religion Sucks 99

spending time with Him. It is good to have a regular devotional time with Jesus, but do not allow that to be the whole sum of the time you spend with Him during the day.

Remember, when you meet with Jesus you are meeting a person not a doctrine or a happy "promise box reading". He is someone who wants to forgive, encourage, reveal, teach and guide you! Ask Him for His presence to visit with you. Listen for His voice and wait for Him to take you away to His secret place so He can speak to you.

The door to this place is passionate worship. Uninhibited. Lavish. Desperate. Extravagant. Wild worship. The kind of worship that lets Jesus into your life and unwraps the spirit of prophecy in your midst!

My favorite encounter of worship in the New Testament is when Mary (the same one who sat at Jesus' feet) wasted an expensive bottle of perfume on the feet of Jesus (John 12:3).

It was a scandalous act. People would talk about this act of worship for hundreds of years. She broke into the acceptable traditions of the day and crossed the lines of what was considered normal and acceptable, because her love for Jesus was so great.

She approached a male guest, interrupted dinner and let her hair down like an immoral woman – each act breaking accepted norms. She then wasted a year's wages ("It could have fed the poor!" – sounds like some religious people today!) on the feet of

Worship Jesus passionately, Uninhabited, Lavish, desperate, Extravagant, wild worship.

Jesus. She dried His feet with her hair. The whole house smelled of perfume!

The smell of passionate worship filled the room and two people walked out of the room smelling the same: Jesus and Mary. That is what worship and hearing the voice of God is all about – smelling like Jesus! I want our worship to be talked about. I want our worship to be scandalous in its sheer abandonment!

If you want to move prophetically, you will continually come up against the religious spirit in your own life and in the lives of others. It will attempt to muffle the sound of God's voice. It will cut you off from intimacy with Jesus. The only remedy is to be sure of God's grace in your life and to pursue Him passionately in worship. If you want to be a significant prophetic voice to this generation, get to know Jesus. He is all prophecy fulfilled. As you get to know Him you will hear Him tell you the secrets of His heart.

But the Lord answered her, "Martha, Martha, you are anxious and troubled about many things, but one thing is necessary. Mary has chosen the good por-tion, which will not be taken away from her." Luke 10:41-42.

In our performance and result-driven society we often overlook the value of relationship in favor of function. Prophetic ministry, by its nature, is forceful and directive. We can, however, misunderstand and misdirect that force. We then reduce the ministry to something functional rather than relational.

God's greatest passion and desire is relationship. He has done everything to make Himself available to us in relationship. When He speaks to us His desire is that we hear His voice from a place of intimacy.

In Amos 3:7 we read,

For the Lord God does nothing without revealing his secret to his servants the prophets.

Secrets are only revealed to those who are trusted. Trust is only developed through intimacy. If you want to hear His voice and prophesy, you'd better get intimate with Jesus. Prophecy is about knowing, feeling and communicating the affections of God's heart. If you want to do that you must experience Jesus. The gift of prophecy is wrapped up in worshipping Jesus.

Then I fell down at his feet to worship him, but he said to me, "You must not do that! I am a fellow servant with you and your brothers who hold to the testimony of Jesus. Worship God." For the testimony of Jesus is the spirit of prophecy. Revelation 19:10 (ESV)

If you want to unwrap this gift you must be found to be a worshipper of God first. Christians have learnt the art of doing before being. In the story of Martha and Mary Jesus said the better part was not serving but sitting at His feet and listening to His voice.

Be a Worshipper of God first !

Intimacy = Trust

I have noticed that our churches are packed with events: prayer meetings, charity drives and the list could go on. All of these are, of course, very important and a necessity in demonstrating the kingdom of God to our communities. But I have found that in the busyness of life we have lost the ability to enjoy God.

Our meetings have become predictable and formalised. Most people can time the worship to their watches and the meeting seems more like a McDonalds drive thru (you know what's on the menu!) rather than a gathering of saints who have come to meet with Jesus.

New Testament church carried with it a sense of unpredictability and wonder. No one seemed to know what would happen next. The church was led by men and women who were sensitive to the Spirit and His leading. They seemed unfazed (and not offended) when the Holy Spirit broke into their meetings. Right from the start of Peter's preaching career God, by His Spirit, interrupted his sermons. Paul had his life revolutionised by God's unexpected breaking in.

When I speak to many Christians the one thing they struggle with is personal time with Jesus. As a result they look to the "man of God" leading them or to another renewal meeting to receive a touch from God. It renders them ineffective for service in God's kingdom because their spiritual tanks are so empty and void of power. It is with this in mind that I want to talk about lingering in the presence of God.

Many books on intimacy, quiet times and devotions so often lead to navel gazing and inward focussed reflection. That's not what lingering is all about. Lingering with God is about faith-filled expectation and revelation. It's about being positioned to experience the indescribable mysteries of heaven. It's about discovering the inexhaustible King of the universe who neither slumbers nor sleeps. It's about God-encounters.

Growing up in a Pentecostal/ Charismatic church was an incredible privilege for me and I have come to enjoy the person of the Holy Spirit so much more because of this. I remember as a young Christian going to meetings where we would "wait for the Spirit" to come. There was a special moment when we all knew that God through the Holy Spirit had stepped into the building. It seemed as if He was more present than before. There was a sense of the immediacy of His presence.

It would always amaze me how many miraculous things happened in that atmosphere. Prophecy was released, people got baptized in the Spirit and spoke in other tongues, people got healed and, most importantly, people got saved. The problem was that these events only took place in big meetings and were centred on one person taking the initiative to "usher in the presence of God". Anyone wishing to experience the nearness of His presence, seemingly could not access this for themselves in his or her day-to-day life.

I remember thinking as a young boy that, surely, if God is everywhere then I can experience Him at home in my room the same way I do in church. I could not and did not want my spiritual life to revolve around a daily devotional and a boring prayer time that did not increase my passion for Jesus.

That was until I read Benny Hinn's book *Good Morning Holy Spirit*. That changed everything for me. Benny Hinn's passion for the Spirit enthused me and I realised that as a son of God the Spirit had been given to me to enjoy intimate fellowship.

1 Corinthains 2:9-12 says,

...no eye has seen, nor ear heard, nor the heart of man imagined, what God has prepared for those who love him – these things God has revealed to us through the Spirit. For the Spirit searches everything, even the depths of God. For who knows a person's thoughts except the spirit of that person, which is in him? So also no one comprehends the thoughts of God except the Spirit of God. Now we have received not the spirit of the world, but the Spirit who is from God, that we might understand the things freely given us by God.

We now have access to the depths of God and the Holy Spirit can reveal the hidden treasures of heaven to us. The aim of the Holy Spirit is to lead us into a more intimate and radical relationship with the Trinity. Mysteries, resources and the will of God are made plain in the person and work of the Spirit.

Jesus said that the Spirit would take what is His and give it to us (John 16:14). All that Christ accomplished at the cross, in the resurrection and in His glorification is now available to us by the Spirit. To *linger* is to access this heavenly realm. The depths of God are inexhaustible and so are the encounters and experiences we can enjoy in Him by the Holy Spirit.

This makes for an exciting life. Joyful contemplation and passionate worship sets the tone for revelation. Most Christians never fully enter into this exciting life because they do not know how much is there for them. The church has watered down the work of the Spirit to a prayer line that happens after a meeting. We have reduced His power to people falling out under the "power of God" and His leading to waiting for goose bumps as confirmation before we make a decision. He is so much more than that!

Visitation or habitation?

Do you not know that you are God's temple and that God's Spirit dwells in you? 1 Corinthians 3:16

God's passionate desire from before the beginning of time was to have intimacy with His people. Right at the genesis of this world God made a garden filled with incredible delights. This garden was covered with amazing diversity and life. It was perfectly ordered and wonderfully creative. This was the context in which God would meet and visit with His created image: His own likeness, His own people.

I find it fascinating that all of the other creatures were simply formed by the word of God, yet when God made Adam there was a detailed intimacy that was attached to His making of man. We see something remarkable happen when God decides to make humans. He stoops down and forms man out of the dust of the earth. Again, God's initiative is to get down low. What amazing mercy! As He does this, He forms man with His own hands (Job 10:8).

There is such a sense of tenderness and focussed intention. Then God does what has not been done to any other created thing. He comes close to man and breathes into his nostrils.

Imagine a holy God coming close and breathing His very life into His own. The most intimate invitation that heaven could offer you was the day He breathed on you and you responded to His salvation!

God's eternal purpose was that He would live amongst His own people and that they would live with Him. God wants to be with us. He wants to dwell with us. God has always wanted to be with His people! In the Garden of Eden he walked with Adam and Eve. He wandered with Israel in a box and a tent, all because He wanted to be with them. He then sent Jesus, the God-Man. God walked the earth in flesh and He was near His people!

Now He dwells in us by His Spirit. He wants to be with us all the time. The problem is that very often we are just happy with a visit! We settle too easily for a one-off experience with God. At best our expectation for Him is really only during extraordinary outpourings of His Spirit.

My pursuit is full possession by the Spirit. I am contending for a habitation of His glory and presence because that is what we were created for. You and I were created to live and move in the realm of His glory. We, however, chose to sin and have fallen from that intimacy and glory. Jesus our mediator is faithful to fill that gap. He lived on earth. He chose to conceal his glory in fleshly clothes so that we could all have access to His presence and glory. God came close again!

The truth is that the Spirit of Jesus still is clothed in humanity. Through the new birth He is able to live in His people by His Spirit. We get to encounter and live in the glory of all that Jesus purchased for us! Jesus promises His disciples that He is going to prepare a place for us.

And if I go and prepare a place for you, I will come again and will take you to myself, that where I am you may be also. John 14:3.

This is not simply talking about mansions in heaven that we receive when we die! Jesus is inviting His disciples to another world. He is inviting us to an intimate place in the Father that is accessed by the Spirit through all that Jesus is.This opens up a whole new realm of revelation and encountering the Father. Think about the great truth found in Ephesians 2:4-6: *But God,* *being rich in mercy, because of the great love with which he loved us, even when we were dead in our trespasses, made us alive together with Christ – by grace – you have been saved and raised us up with him and seated with him in the heavenly places in Christ Jesus.*

These are not mere theological truths that have no bearing on us today. This is a present and positional reality. We can live from heaven's perspective and walk as strangers and aliens in this world!

Intimacy with Jesus has a knock-on effect. It draws us into a radical encounter with the Father. It's amazing the heights and depths to which we are called. This is not for those who are prophetic only; it is an invitation to all who are called sons. We can live in the place of His presence and enjoy the resources of heaven twenty-four-seven.

Many Christians live an impoverished spiritual life because they do not know that they have access to the Fathers' house. We live like the older brother in the story of the prodigal son: always working yet never enjoying the fathers' provision.

A place is prepared for you in the Father's house. It's a place of intimacy and revelation. It's a place of lives changed and destiny fulfilled. You can go there any time. Jesus has gone ahead of you and made the way open. You can access heavenly realms any time, in any place. He wants to "tabernacle" (make a dwelling place) with you. That's the place that revelation will flow from.

I believe we are to be a people who carry the presence of God! The purpose of the tabernacle was a foreshadowing of what Jesus would accomplish through the new covenant. The Spirit of Jesus would dwell in a temple not made by human hands, but by God Himself. God told the Levites in the Old Testament that

* You can access heavenly realms any time, in any place

they were to "carry" the Ark of the Covenant. This is am amazing picture for us today.

This tribe was set apart to do one thing only: make sure that the Ark of the Covenant was carried appropriately (Deuteronomy 10:8).

They had no portion in any inheritance. No land that they could own. No access to the provision that the other Israelites had. They were to be set apart for the sole task of carrying the presence of God. Their reward was the privilege of having God as their inheritance. He says to this tribe, "I will be your reward." Everything else seems like fake costume jewellery in comparison to having Him. The invitation we get is to have unlimited access to the Creator of all things. Our reward as Christians is free access into the very presence and power of God!

Silence is Golden

The truth about seeking God is that even when He is silent, there are lessons to be learned. Most Christians respond to God's silence as an indicator that He is not with them, when actually it is an opportunity for faith.

Another aspect to prophetic ministry is what we do during the season when God goes silent! Part of the prophetic ministry is about seeking after Him. Often heaven will go silent on us and we will have to press into God without sensing His presence and anointing. This is often a difficult time and can cause a prophetic person much frustration. If we can see this as an opportunity to

Even when God is silent, there are lessons to be learned.

learn more about God, however, then we will see it work out for our good. As I wrote earlier, God hides Himself for us, not from us. His heart lights up with joy when He sees us get excited about seeking Him out and finding Him.

Today if you are in a difficult situation and can't hear God's voice, keep focused on what you know to be true about Him. Keep worshipping Him. Keeping seeking after Him. Because you will be found by Him! Seek God's heart and learn to live in grace. Avoid the trap of lifeless religion. All fruit springs from the place of natural, unforced intimacy with Jesus. He loves you!

God hides himself for us, not from us.
His heart lights up with Joy when he sees
us excited about seeking him out and
finding him.

7
What To Do While You Wait

This charge I entrust to you, Timothy, my child, in accordance with the prophecies previously made about you, that by them you may wage the good warfare, holding faith and a good conscience. By rejecting this some have made a shipwreck of their faith.
1 Timothy 1:18-19

Leonard Ravenhill said, "An opportunity of a lifetime must be seized in the lifetime of the opportunity."

When you begin to understand that God's nature in the Bible is often revealed as a wise farmer, you'll understand something about the way He works with your prophetic destiny.

Gods nature — Wise farmer
Good farmer

The nature of God's kingdom is often described in farming terms. God is the farmer of this world and we are His sons, sown into this world as seeds to reflect Him and impact the world around us. He allows the wheat and tares to grow together, so the only way we'll know the difference is when they mature. A tare has an empty head and stands tall, whereas wheat has a head full of reproductive seed with the potential to multiply and is bowed low (Matthew 13:24-30).

God, being a good farmer, works in season and deals with us in this context. It's important to realise this because many miss the day of their prophetic breakthrough simply because they have not understood the ways of God. To everything there is a season, Ecclesiastes says, and all things, no matter what they look like right now, become beautiful in their time.

There are two concepts of "time" in the Bible. There is *chronos* time which is measured time i.e. from 1 until 4 o'clock. Then there is time that works within time – *kairos* time. Kairos time is a moment in time, an opportune time for action.

When the Bible says in Colossians 4:5 that we must *"redeem the time"* Paul is not talking about managing our diaries better. He is saying that there are set times in which God seems to work. When we recognize and take hold of those *kairos moments* we will often get a whole lot more than we bargained for!

Jesus came at a kairos time, when the moment in God's season was just right. This was the "time" that Jesus told the Pharisees

✳ Two concepts of time in the Bible:
chronos: 1 to 4 oclock
kairos: moment in time, opportune time for action

they had missed. He came at the set time, in the fullness of time, yet the Pharisees completely missed their prophetic inheritance because of their inability to see what God was doing in their midst.

Many Christians have received prophetic promises. We are required to respond to and "pick up" these words. The nature of prophetic revelation is powerful when understood and walked in. I know too many people who have received words, written them down and put them in their book of promises without ever walking in them.

Worse still, others go looking for prophetic words that will confirm their plans, rather than finding a revelation of God's heart. Many prophetic conferences are filled to capacity, but people walk away disappointed or even offended by the man or woman of God who did not give them a personal word.

The nature of the prophetic word is to give us a glimpse, to open a window into our purpose and destiny in God – it's not intended to confirm the already decided plans of our heart.

God's plan for me and you is more than salvation and a one-way ticket to heaven. He has purposes for us that have been spoken of before the foundation of time. We can either walk in them or ignore and miss them.

The prophetic creates what the call of God requires. It acts as a pioneering force to open to us that which is closed and shut up.

Thats why the Bible tells us that the prophetic word is like a light in a dark place. The nature of a kingdom word creates the reality it proclaims. It opens your destiny to you.

Matthew 16 it tells us that *revelation* acts as a key to the kingdom. Jesus is talking about the revelation that came to Peter from the Father and goes onto to say that *the keys of the kingdom* come to us in the context of such revelation.

These are keys of authority that are released by revelation. This explains why we only experience spiritual victory in areas where we have revelation. In other words, we will never step out in healing until we have a revelation of God's love and compassion. We will never have authority over our finances until we get the revelation of generosity. Revelation releases keys of authority. This is true of prophetic revelation. Prophecy is an invitation into an encounter with heavenly purposes.

Many people live outside of their prophetic destiny and never inherit the promises of God. I have noticed that people tend to view prophecy either as fatalism or a serving suggestion. It is neither. As a result, people get disappointed or angry with God. Hope deferred makes the heart sick, the Bible says, and often people live with diseased hearts because they have never understood God's purpose in their lives.

God is more interested in your relationship with Him than you waiting for His commands. Prophetic revelation is a two-way street. It is relational. It is God dreaming with us. We get

Prophetic is 2 way street
1. Relational
2 God dreaming with us

to partner with Him. Remember, God has not made you to be a robot – He made you a son or daughter and therefore your interaction with His promises are required for them to be fulfilled!

Sometimes people delay their prophetic promises by not learning how to lean into them. When the Bible says we are to "weigh" the prophetic, it is not just telling us to judge whether a particular word is from God or not. Metaphorically we need to put our weight into it! We are called to significantly expect and believe that God wants to do what He has said.

The nature of the prophetic is to inspire hope, which when fulfilled becomes a tree of life. Therefore, the key to seeing increased prophetic activity is celebrating what God has already done in accomplishing His words through and in you.

I have an expectation that the word of the Lord will come to pass because I have already seen enough past words fulfilled, beginning with my call to salvation. I therefore expect Him to keep on speaking and acting.

We need to understand what it means to *"wage the good warfare"* (1 Timothy 1:18) to possess the prophetic revelation we have received.

There are some things I have learnt which have helped me in pursuing the fulfilment of the words spoken over me. I want to say clearly as I mention some keys to unlocking destiny, that

Jesus is the fulfilment of all prophecy. He is the beginning and the end. On the mount of transfiguration we see Jesus as the fulfilment of both the Law, Moses and the prophets and Elijah. They all come together in Him.

Our pursuit therefore must be one that sees Him at the centre of it all. When we pursue Jesus, all the promises get released. The Bible says that in Jesus all of the promises of God are Yes and amen. He is our great amen. He is the one who says "and so be it."

Paul, in his letter to Timothy, reminded him of the prophetic words he received at his ordination as an elder (1 Timothy 1:18). It's important to see the weight Paul puts on this. These words are so weighty to Paul that they act as a compass in the seas of adversity.

That's what the prophetic does, it directs you. It helps you to avoid shipwreck. It is so important to remind yourself of the words spoken over you. This way the promises of God remain fresh in your mind and in your heart. The prophetic word contains keys to help you fight.

Brothers and sisters, let's not be ignorant. The devil, our adversary, is like a lion seeking whom he may devour. We are involved in spiritual warfare by virtue of the fact that we are born again. But we have joy in the fact that God speaks His word over us in order to establish us in His will for our lives.

Get into the word or clothe ourselves in the word.

When Paul says to "wage a good warfare" by the prophetic word, he means that we should literally "get into" the word or clothe ourselves with the word. The word acts like protective armour as we pursue our destiny. Get into your words from God, get into your promises from Him. Timothy had received certain promises over his life. He was instructed to get into them, not leave them on the shelf.

So is my Word that goes out from my mouth: It will not return to me empty, but will accomplish what I desire and achieve the purpose for which I sent it. Isaiah 55:11

Timothy had received certain words from the team that laid hands on him. These were keys to his destiny and Paul commends Timothy earlier in this chapter for his stand against those who would teach a gospel contrary to the gospel of grace. He had to be confident in his prophetic call to fight some of this stuff.

In the DNA of prophetic words spoken over you are the keys to fight for your destiny. It's so important to record those words and to highlight the truth in them regarding how God sees you.

When the enemy throw curves balls at you, you can confidently say, "That's not true!"

Prophetic words should always pull out of you who you really are in the light of the finished work of Jesus. They always should point to your redemptive purpose in God.

The primary way the enemy will get us to "shipwreck" our destiny is to distort truth and rock our faith. Notice Paul uses this sailing metaphor to illustrate his point. In those days sailors operated primarily by faith in their compass. The compass told them which way they were going. If their compass was out, or there was some other magnetic interference, that would pretty much be game-over for them.

What is to be our guide, Paul says, is faith and a good conscience. Faith is active. While we are waiting for our breakthrough, we are not called to passivity, but to active faith. We are to "put on" our prophetic word and step into it.

Faith trusts in God to release us into who we are called to be, and then actively walks towards that destiny. A good conscience is one that holds us and steers us clear of anything that would detract from the purity and beauty of God's call on our life.

It means that our decision making in life can be pure and faith-filled. This is why God calls us to posture ourselves like children in order to access his kingdom. Purity, simplicity and faith in the goodness of God.

The prophetic word reveals something about you and your destiny. It carries a revelation of how God sees you and the redemptive purpose He has for you in changing the world. It is very important that you understand this as it will help you fight.

The prophetic unlocks your identity as heaven sees you. This is helpful for a number of reasons. It builds faith in you, it places courage in you and it directs you. Paul reminded Timothy of the gifts he had and then prophesied into his destiny by saying,

For God gave us a spirit not of fear but of power and love and self-control. 2 Timothy 1:7

Power, Love, self-control.

He re-aligned Timothy's understanding of himself.

The key ingredient in activating the prophetic is *agreement*. First you weigh the word, which simply means evaluating the word and making sure it is biblical, carries revelation and produces faith in you. Those around you who know you and care for you will often know and be able to help in this process. Then once this is done the process of doing warfare with your word begins.

Agree with God, and be at peace; thereby good will come to you. Job 22:21

Believe in the Lord your God, and you will be established; believe his prophets, and you will succeed. 1 Chronicles 20:20

Again I say to you, if two of you agree on earth about anything they ask, it will be done for them by my Father in heaven. Matthew 18:19

The word "agree" means a number of different things. Each of these verse makes a point about how we are to receive and believe the prophetic word. In the book of Job the word agree means "to acquaint yourself with God". I am praying more and more that I learn to "know" God not just know about Him. When you know Him and you are acquainted with Him, any words you receive are connected to His character and it is easy to tell whether or not they are trustworthy.

Believe. To Trust God

The word "believe" in 2 Chronicles 20:20 simply means to "trust God". Thats all there is to it. Trust must always come from the place of rest – knowing that because He is good He is working all things for my good and His glory!

In Matthew 18:19 the word for agree is where we get the word "symphony". It speaks of many different sounds coming together to make one big sound. The implication is that when we agree with God we release the power of heaven's sound to break open the reality of heaven on earth.

What you "agree" with will release power in your life. In fact, this is the primary way that the enemy gain access into our lives. It is through agreements, conscious or unconsciously made with him. But the Bible is clear that all authority has been given to Jesus. The devil has no authority. There is a difference between authority and power. Authority is the permission to act. Power is the ability to act.

Although the devil has power to act, his authority was stripped away at the cross on a hill called Golgotha. Golgotha means "the place of the skull". The primary entrance point for spiritual warfare is in the area of the mind. Until we replace the words of the devil with kingdom words we will live in a place of despair and brokenness, rather than allowing our prophetic words to shape our destiny.

There are some reading this who have laid down their prophetic destiny. I'm here to tell you it is time to do some warfare! It is time for hope to be restored. Get into you word, use it as truth to fight the enemy.

In 2 Kings 13 we see the story of King Joash coming to Elisha the prophet for a word from God concerning the battle he was to fight against the Syrians. We see the prophet tell him to open a window and shoot an arrow of the Lord's deliverance right into Aphek, which means "stronghold or fortress". The word of the Lord carries power. Aim to fire it right into the stronghold of the enemy.

The prophet tells the king to take the arrows and strike the ground with them. He only does this a few times and Elisha gets angry with him saying, "If you would have struck the ground more times you would have defeated the enemy."

Too many give up just before their breakthrough! Pulverise those arrows into the ground. The Bible says that the arrow of the Lord will go forth like lightning (Zechariah 9:14). The Bible describes arrows as words that can be used for destruction.

Where are you aiming your arrows? Against the enemy or people? They carry an ability to destroy the enemy or people.

Spiritual warfare is not meant to be enemy-focused but promise-focused! When we fight against the attempts of the enemy to rob us of the purposes of God, we do it in the security of God's goodness towards us.

He who did not spare his own Son but gave him up for us all, how will he not also with him graciously give us all things? Romans 8:32

In conclusion then, if we are to walk into our destiny we need to be a a people of clear conscience, faith and agreement. God's plan for us is that we walk into our destiny as a friend and son, not as a slave. He tells us His secrets (Psalm 25:1) and provides the ability to walk into it all!

Suggested Reading List

Growing in the Prophetic, Mike Bickle (Creation House, 1996)

The Prophetic Ministry, Rick Joyner (Morning Star, 1997)

The Voice of God, Cindy Jacobs (Regal, 1995,1997)

Surprised by the Voice of God, Jack Deere (Zondervan, 1996, 1998)

Surprised by the Power of Spirit, Jack Deere (Zondervan, 1994)

The Beginner's Guide to the Gift of Prophecy, Jack Deere (Vine Books, 2001)

Prophetic Etiquette, Michael Sullivant (Creation House, 2000)

Dream Language, Jim W. Goll (Destiny Image, 2006)

About the author

Having grown up in Cape Town, South Africa, Julian Adams relocated to the UK in 2008 with a sense of call to see churches grow in the dimension of supernatural ministry. Julian travels extensively both in the UK and internationally, serving many churches, equipping the church to hear God's voice, receiving words of knowledge and healing the sick. He's an  experienced prophet with a strong teaching gift and has a passion to see the whole church mobilised to bring the kingdom of God onto the streets. Julian serves various apostolic streams and people have described his gift as extremely accurate and his insights into building the church as invaluable.

Julian established The Frequentsee Trust in 2011. The Frequentsee Trust serves to demonstrate and raise up authentic prophetic ministry in the church. At the heart of Frequentsee is a desire to see men and women mentored and released with a clear call to extend God's kingdom in every context of the world. The Trust is increasingly in demand to help build a culture of the supernatural in local churches alongside biblical, apostolic ministry. The Trust is also involved in helping bring justice and mercy alongside various ministries across the nations. Frequentsee offers training, mentoring, prophetic consultation and opportunities for mission in the developing world.

FREQUENTSEE

Contact details:

website: www.frequentsee.org

email: admin@frequentsee.org

Please note that I will not respond to emails requesting a prophetic word. Whilst I love prophesying over people, it is best done in the context of a local church where it can be weighed. He loves you with an everlasting love!

Easter   ↗ no children

2 Services: 9:00 am, 11 am

Easter egg?